The Cultural W〜 〜phets

The Cultural World of the Prophets

The First Reading and the Responsorial Psalm

Sunday by Sunday,
Year C

John J. Pilch

LITURGICAL PRESS
Collegeville, Minnesota

www.litpress.org

Year B: ISBN 0-8146-2787-0
Year C: ISBN 0-8146-2788-9

2	3	4	5	6	7	8	9

Library of Congress Cataloging-in-Publication Data

Pilch, John J.
    The cultural world of the prophets: the first reading and the responsorial psalm / John J. Pilch.
        p. cm.
    Includes bibliographical references.
    Contents: Sunday by Sunday, Year B.
    ISBN 0-8146-2787-0 (alk. paper)
    1. Bible. O.T.–Criticism, interpretation, etc. 2. Bible. O.T.–History of biblical events. 3. Middle East–Civilization–To 622. 4. Catholic Church. Lectionary for Mass (U.S.). Year C. I. Title.

BS1171.3.P55 2002
264'.34–dc21

                                                          2002028667

For Professor T. R. Hobbs
Hamilton, Ontario, Canada

Faithful friend
and colleague
in the Word

Contents

Introduction

When I wrote *The Cultural World of Jesus: Sunday by Sunday* (3 vols., The Liturgical Press, 1995–1997), I resolved to write a companion series: *The Cultural World of the Apostles: The Second Reading, Sunday by Sunday* (3 vols., The Liturgical Press, 2001–2003). My intention was to provide the average person with a handy study guide, first for the gospel readings, then later for the second readings in the liturgy every Sunday, which are drawn chiefly from letters. Since it was becoming—and still is—difficult for adults to find some free time during the week to attend a study group or lecture series on the Bible, I thought that a six-hundred-word essay on the Scripture heard at liturgy on Sunday could be manageable and interesting. A person could read that while sitting in the pew before the liturgy began. If the homily wasn't working out well, a person could read the reflection in its place.

That the booklets have been useful for preachers, catechists, liturgists, and others as well came as a pleasant and welcome surprise. My publisher's suggestion to write a series on the first readings in the liturgy Sunday by Sunday, *The Cultural World of the Prophets*, also came as a surprise. The gospels and the second readings in Sunday liturgies present selections in a continuous or semi-continuous sequence that facilitates an orderly study of a gospel or a letter of an apostle Sunday by Sunday.

In contrast, the selection and arrangement of the first readings in Sunday liturgies do not lend themselves to a similar study program. Yet the Old Testament passages are of significance in Christian worship. With this volume I turn to the task of offering insight into these Old Testament passages, a task of interest to me since graduate school. At the beginning of the second year in my first teaching position, after completing my degree with a specialty in the New Testament (the letters of Paul), the dean asked if I could teach Old Testament courses. If not, my year-to-year contract would not be renewed, since he had just hired a Harvard graduate to teach New Testament and now needed someone to teach Old Testament. Well, of course I could teach the Old Testament! My graduate training at Marquette University was quite broad compared to other institutions. My Old Testament teachers included J. Coert Rylersdaam, Roland Murphy, O.CARM., Robert North, S.J., Thomas Caldwell, S.J., John F. X. Sheehan, S.J., and Gordon Bahr, among others. An article I published in *Harvard Theological Review* as a graduate student critically reviewed a scholarly study of Martin Luther's Commentaries on the Psalms. In all the years that have passed since beginning the serious study of Scripture, I have maintained a balanced interest in the entire Bible.

As a rule, the first reading—mainly though not always from the Old Testament—has been chosen in order to harmonize, in a more or less explicit way, with the doctrine and events recounted in the gospel. At times the connection is very slim, and in addition to that, the selections are drawn from all over the Old Testament. Except for the Sundays of Easter, the readings are neither continuous nor semi-continuous. Biblical scholars and liturgists have lamented that the Old Testament does not get a fair hearing in the liturgy. From a modern, historically oriented point of view, this is correct. The gospel controls the selection of the first reading in Sunday liturgies. There is no escaping the impression that the gospel is considered more important in our worship service. That conviction, however, has some ancient roots. Theodore Abu Qurrah, Bishop of Haran (died ninth century C.E.), the town from where Abraham departed for Canaan, wrote:

> Were it not for the Gospel, we would not have acknowledged Moses to be from God. Rather, on reflection, we would have vigorously opposed him. Likewise, we have acknowledged the prophets to be from God because of the

Gospel. It is not on the basis of reason, since we have acknowledged them because Christ has informed us that they are prophets. Also, because we have knowledge of Christ's whole economy, and having read their books and discovered that they had previously described his whole economy just as he accomplished it, we have acknowledged that they are prophets. At this point in time we do not acknowledge Christ and his affairs because of the books of the prophets. Rather, we acknowledge them because of Christ's saying that they are prophets and because of our own recognition that his economy is written in their books.[1]

Just as in the volumes of my other *The Cultural World of . . .* series, here too I present the reader with a thumbnail sketch of the literary context and historical setting of each Scripture text-segment as it contributes to understanding the selected verses. I also present cultural information, at length when necessary (for example, see the discussion of Genesis 18:1-10a on the Sixteenth Sunday in Ordinary Time), which is indispensable for understanding those verses appropriately and which is usually unavailable in other commentaries or resources. That kind of cultural information is what has made this series distinctive. I include similar brief reflections on the Responsorial Psalm, and for each Sunday I indicate the apparent link ("more or less explicit") by which the gospel should be associated with the first reading. There may indeed be links or associations other than those I have indicated. Finally, the Sundays marked with an asterisk (*) were assigned readings that are repeated in each year of the lectionary cycle. I will repeat these reflections substantially unchanged in the other volumes of this series just as I did in the volumes of the previous series.

I am grateful to the Liturgical Press for publishing and promoting my cultural reflections and to the readers around the world who continue to welcome and to benefit from these

---

[1] Quoted from Bruce J. Malina, "Three Theses for a More Adequate Reading of the New Testament," *Practical Theology: Perspectives from the Plains,* ed. Michael G. Lawler and Gail S. Risch (Omaha: Creighton University Press, 2000) 33–60.

publications. I believe that together we all have taken some important steps toward realizing a goal that I set for myself upon completing my graduate studies: to contribute toward improving preaching.

Feast of Saint Francis of Assisi   John J. Pilch
October 4, 2002   Georgetown University
                                    and University of Pretoria,
                                              South Africa
                         and Studium Bilicum Franciscanum,
                                               Hong Kong

First Sunday of Advent
Jeremiah 33:14-16

The Old Testament readings for the season of Advent are prophecies about the Messiah and the age that the Messiah will inaugurate. Scholars agree that in this chapter an editor has reworked Jeremiah's earlier oracle about a future king. In Jeremiah 23:5-6, the prophet announces to Judah (under siege in 587 B.C.E.) that God will raise a new, righteous king ("a just shoot") to replace Zedekiah, a puppet king. This new king will do "what is right and just in the land." To do what is right *(mišpat)* means to impose one's will upon others, that is, an authority who acts in this way should judge fairly and correctly in any given situation. To do what is just *(ṣedaqa)* describes a person who does exactly what the situation calls for. Such a one is ever blameless in the sight of God, like Noah and Abraham.

Now in Mediterranean societies of antiquity, including that of our ancestors in the faith, there was not the faintest trace of human equality, whether in the eyes of the law or even in some vague ideal of equality. Everyone tried to take advantage of others, that is, relationships were exploitive. Jeremiah's oracle, therefore, announces that God will raise a king the likes of which they have never experienced before. The king will behave after the fashion of God: justly and rightly. Good as this news would be to people who never experienced righteousness and justice in their lives, it was no doubt welcome but received with skepticism. The editor's reworking of Jeremiah's earlier oracle replaces Israel (Jer 23:6) with Jerusalem (Jer 33:16), which is given the same name as the king: "Yahweh is my righteousness," with the emphasis on YHWH!

Jeremiah's oracle tallies well with the gospel which tells of a final reckoning. Everyone, but especially authorities, particularly those who rule in God's name, had better be able to prove that they have done what is right and just in the land.

Responsorial Psalm: 25:4-5, 8-9, 10, 14

Dating probably from the post-exilic period (around 450 B.C.E.), the verses selected from this acrostic lament of a collectivistic personality (one who finds identity in the group) for today's response offer his prayerful plea that Jeremiah's promise be realized: "He [YHWH] guides the humble [*anawim*, plural] to justice [*mišpat*, that is, to do what is right]" (v. 9). Notice how the author of this lament speaks of himself in the singular (make known to me; teach me, my savior, I wait, etc.), but slips readily, quickly, and easily into the plural: "he shows sinners the way." This is the sure sign of a collectivistic personality, not a Western individual. The collectivistic plurals appear also in Jesus' exhortations to his disciples (Luke 21:25-28, 34-36).

Second Sunday of Advent
Baruch 5:1-9

Baruch, a royal scribe (Jer 36:26, 32), has often been called Jeremiah's "secretary" and amanuensis. (Recall that only 2 percent of ancient populations were literate.) Baruch and Jeremiah were indeed contemporaries and friends. He wrote the first Jeremiah scroll as the prophet dictated it (Jer 36:4). Jeremiah tried to assuage Baruch's disappointment that he might never receive personal fame and recognition by delivering an oracle from the Lord saying Baruch should be grateful that his life will be spared in the coming cataclysm (Jeremiah 45)! King Johoiakim burned the first Jeremiah scroll, so the prophet dictated another to Baruch. Ironically, contemporary scholars agree that Baruch is probably NOT the author of the book of Baruch! Though this collection of material is set in the context of the fall of Jerusalem in 587 B.C.E., the actual date of composition is probably between 300 B.C.E. and prior to 70 C.E., long after Jeremiah and Baruch died.

Baruch 4:5–5:9 constitute one piece, and today's verses (5:1-9) are spoken by the prophet to Jerusalem. These are words of comfort ("take off your robe of mourning and misery"); the exiles are returning ("God will bring them back to you"). Jerusalem receives new names from God: "the peace of justice" and the "glory of God's worship." (There is no Hebrew text for Baruch, but the Greek [Septuagint] word for justice is the one that translates the Hebrew *mišpat*–as on the First Sunday of Advent.) Jerusalem will experience the peace that derives from "doing what is right!" Peace and justice will prevail forever. God, who leads Israel from exile back to Jerusalem, guides them with divine mercy and justice *(mišpat)*. Just as John the Baptist (Luke 3:4) cites Isaiah (40:3-5) to encourage his listeners to prepare a smooth path for the Lord, so does Baruch observe that God personally will prepare a smooth road for the returnees, concepts that help link these readings.

Responsorial Psalm: 126:1-2, 2-3, 4-5, 6

Sung at the New Year, this psalm reflects the sentiments of Israelites who would look back at the old year and realize how often and in how many ways they had failed God. Indeed, the backward glance frequently involved a view of misfortunes, reversals, scorn by nations, and even exile. Now that the fortunes are reversed, the restored Israelites can hardly believe it! Their enemies have been forced to admit that "their God has [finally!!] done great things for them." These verses serve as a fitting link between the Old Testament reading and today's gospel (Luke 3:1-6), both of which speak of a very new and redemptive thing that the Lord is already beginning to do.

Third Sunday of Advent
Zephaniah 3:14-18a

Zephaniah, who traced his lineage back to King Hezekiah (715–687 B.C.E.; see Zeph 1:1), prophesied in the days of King Josiah (640–609 B.C.E.), who attempted to initiate serious reform in Judah. This explains why he does not criticize the king along with other segments of society that the prophet condemns. Assyria, who conquered Israel in 721 B.C.E., is tottering on the verge of collapse to the rising Babylonian power. The identification of the prophet and his historical circumstances reminds us, as Benedictine scholar Thomas P. Wahl has noted, that "the prophetic word is no perennial religious truth, but a message addressed to a specific moment in history" (*New Jerusalem Biblical Commentary* 17:3).

These verses selected for today's reading sound an exhortation to rejoice that continues to the end of the book of Zephaniah (3:20). The reason for rejoicing is that the Lord is in the midst of Jerusalem, and that divine presence assures victory or successful escape from certain conquest in an attack. This selection can be linked with Luke's report in today's gospel (3:15) that "the people were filled with expectation." Salvation, rescue is on the immediate horizon!

Responsorial Psalm: Isaiah 12:2-3, 4, 5-6

These verses from Isaiah actually reflect the style of psalms, especially psalms of narrative praise sometimes incorrectly–from a cultural point of view–called "individual psalms of thanksgiving." Individualism as it is prized in Western culture doesn't exist in collectivistic cultures such as that of our ancestors in the faith. While the author of these verses says, *"I am confident; . . . my* strength . . . is the LORD," etc., the switch to the plural ("you will draw water") is typical of collectivistic persons who draw their identity from the group, are reluctant to stand out from the group, and disappear into the group as soon as possible.

The phrase "my savior" appears twice in our reading and three times in verses 1 through 6. The Hebrew behind savior, *yešuʿa,* is Jesus' name in Hebrew. While Jesus is not explicitly named in today's gospel (Luke 3:10-18), John the Baptist refers to him indirectly ("one mightier than I").

Isaiah's verses form a fitting bridge between the first reading and the gospel. The verses recognize God as savior and then express praise and indebtedness for a favor received which is the culturally normal response to a gift from a patron in the Mediterranean world. Zephaniah and Luke both describe incredible gifts from God (rescue; a Messiah) and the only fitting response is to sing the praises of the gift giver, God! The response makes that quite clear.

Fourth Sunday of Advent
Micah 5:1-4a

Micah probably preached during the last years of Ahaz or later (around 725–700 B.C.E.). He used the fall of Samaria (721 B.C.E.) as an example to Jerusalem. The prophet lived in turbulent times. Jerusalem had been besieged in 701 B.C.E. People syncretistically worshiped Canaanite deities alongside YHWH. Bribery was rife. Micah is concerned with the people's abandonment of God, and his reputation as a prophet of doom outlived him (Jer 26:18-19, a hundred years later).

But he also delivered a message of hope such as that reflected in today's verses. The historical context is that Jerusalem is being invaded, and the present king is ineffective. He is being shamed. When the mother of the new king gives birth (5:3), God will reverse Jerusalem's fortunes. This new king will be a "new" David (Bethlehem is the city of Jesse and his son David). The rest of the king's kindred will return from exile. Eventually this king will be crowned and rule in the name and with the strength of the Lord. When Assyria is conquered, peace will ensue, and this king's reputation will extend "to the ends of the earth." This uplifting promise to frustrated people in the eighth century B.C.E., inadequately realized at that time, finds eventual fulfillment in the "one who is to give birth" featured in today's gospel (Luke 1:39-45). Luke's audience would readily appreciate this Davidic allusion just as Micah's audience recognized his allusions to classical Messianic sentiments: Isaiah 7; 9; 11; 2 Samuel 7; Psalm 89.

Responsorial Psalm: 80:2-3, 15-16, 18-19

This is one of the very few psalms that had its origin in Israel, the northern kingdom (v. 1). It can be dated no earlier than 721 B.C.E., the fall of the northern kingdom. The tribes of the northern kingdom are the sons of Joseph (Ephraim and Manasseh, Gen 49:12-15) and Joseph's brother, Benjamin. The meaning of Benjamin in Hebrew is "son of my right hand," and the psalmist cleverly introduces this in verse 18. (In ancient Israel, the proof of manliness was not only the ability to endure suffering and pain without shrieking but also mastery of language.)

The psalm is a national lament. Israel has fallen! The refrain of today's responsorial psalm is actually verse 4 of the psalm, in which it is repeated three (four?) times: verses 4, 8, [15?], 20. "Turn to you" is often translated "convert" or "conversion." The community asks God to help in its efforts to return to God so as to undo the tragedy. To stir God to action, the psalmist addresses the deity with a very ancient honorific title: Shepherd [of the flock of Joseph] (Gen 49:24). Then he introduces an allegory (v. 9: "vine"), which he extends throughout the psalm. It appears in today's verses: God, look down from heaven and see your vine! Confidence in God's positive response evokes the promise: "We will no more withdraw from you . . . we will call upon your name." These sentiments of "conversion" and a promise of a renewed life link the good news of both the first reading and the gospel rather well.

* Vigil of the Nativity
Isaiah 62:1-5

These verses appear to capture the prophet's meditation on chapters that Second Isaiah, his master, had composed (Isaiah 40; 51; 54). In these verses Third Isaiah sings about Israel rising to new life from its destruction. The imagery that dominates these verses is drawn from espousals. Zion/Jerusalem's good fortune will break forth as suddenly and brightly as a desert dawn. In antiquity, deities often wore a crown that imitated the walls of their city on earth. Here God is holding such a crown; God is indeed in charge of this glorious restoration. One of the names by which the city once could be described ("Forsaken") is the name of a queen-mother (ʿazuba, 1 Kings 22:42). Cities were considered to be feminine. The new names carry similar symbolism. For example, "My Delight" *(ḥepṣi-bah)* is another queen-mother (2 Kings 21:1), but the names portray a reversal of destiny. The forsaken woman (city) is now God's delight. This is especially evident in the name "Espoused" *(beʿula),* which forgets Israel's whoring ways as described by Hos 2:18.

In this culture, an unfaithful wife would have to be set aside or killed (see Num 5:11-31; Deut 22:13-21). The ideal marriage partner is a patrilateral cousin. What if there is no other available female cousin to replace the unfaithful partner? The man would have to remain unmarried and alone. In the real world of this culture, it is preferable to swallow one's pride, bear the shame, and keep the faithless partner than to be absolutely correct but lose one's partner. So, too, with

9

God. Since all God-talk is based upon and rooted in human experience culturally conditioned, God can be expected to swallow pride, put up with the disappointment, and, as the prophet says, "as a young man married a virgin, / your Builder shall marry you."

The link to the gospel (Matt 1:1-25) is rather clear. Joseph knew Mary was pregnant, and he knew that he was not the father. He would be a thief to claim the child, but Joseph was a holy man who strove to please God always. God's messenger assures Joseph that keeping Mary as his spouse is God's plan for him. In Matthew's genealogy, the four women who appear are non-Israelites and some are of dubious character, yet each won a place in God's plan. These women possess "acquired honor," thus making Jesus completely honorable since his ancestors in his genealogy possess both ascribed and acquired honor.

Responsorial Psalm: 89:4-5, 16-17, 27, 29

We return again to other verses from this lament. The refrain in particular is a most appropriate response to Third Isaiah's insight. Mention of God's "countenance" brings to mind not only the Temple where Israel went "to see" God, but also Moses' experience at Mount Sinai, and other instances which made God's presence very palpable in the mighty deeds God worked for the chosen people. The final verse repeats a familiar adoption-formula often sung at the coronation of new kings (see Psalm 2). Indeed, God will remain loyal to this son-king forever; the covenant with him will remain unshaken.

* Nativity: Midnight Mass
Isaiah 9:1-6

Earlier in the book of Isaiah, we heard the prophet's oracle looking for a successor to Ahaz, in whom God's promise of a lasting destiny would be realized (Isa 7:14-15). In this chapter, Isaiah describes that successor (possibly Hezekiah, ca. 716 B.C.E.) who ascended to the throne upon his father's death (2 Kgs 16:20). The first four verses today express hope for deliverance of the northern kingdom. The words "yoke," "pole," and "rod" refer to Assyrian domination even before 721 B.C.E., and the verses express hopes that YHWH would deliver Israel from the Assyrians. It is difficult for someone who has never lived under an occupying military power to appreciate how conquered people yearn for independence. Anyone who could deliver a nation from such a condition would be a welcome leader.

Verses 5-6 are a triumphant coronation hymn composed by Isaiah for Hezekiah, the son of God's promise in Isaiah 7:14. Wonder-counselor means this king will not need advisers such as those who led his father astray. God-Hero is a mighty warrior designation. Father-Forever describes the quality of his rule (see Prov 31:8-9), and peace results because of the king's abilities, because God promised it, and because judgment and justice now sustain the dynasty. When Hezekiah did not meet the expectations expressed in these verses and in the previous oracle (7:10-17), Isaiah projected his hopes to a later time (11:1-9). This evening's gospel (Luke 2:1-14) identifies Jesus as the one who fulfills these hopes magnificently: he is Messiah and Lord.

11

Responsorial Psalm: 96:1-2, 2-3, 11-12, 13

This is an enthronement psalm that honors God as Israel's king. Today's verses are selected from the first call to praise (vv. 1-3) and the second set of reasons given for this praise (vv. 10-13). The author of this psalm has borrowed heavily from other composers (Psalms 33; 91; 98; and Isa 42:10). The word "announce" (his salvation) is a Hebrew word from which the English word "gospel" derives. This psalmist's inspiration prompts him to broaden the vision of Second Isaiah to a more universal sweep than Isaiah imagined: The Lord shall rule not just Israel but all the earth.

* Nativity: Mass at Dawn
Isaiah 62:11-12

Third Isaiah seeks to prevent two unfortunate choices in post-exilic Jerusalem: that the people will lose hope and settle for less than God has promised, or that they will keep high hopes and become frustrated. These concluding verses of a section proclaiming salvation for a glorious new daughter Zion (Isa 60:1–62:12) string together three up-lifting titles: holy people; redeemed of the LORD; and "frequented," that is, a city that is not forgotten but rather visited by its Savior and recognized by all nations. In the accompanying gospel (Luke 2:15-20), after visiting Joseph, Mary, and the infant, the shepherds announce all that had been told to them about Jesus. Third Isaiah's vision for Zion is realized in the birth of Jesus.

Responsorial Psalm: 97:1, 6, 11-12

Another post-exilic psalm which honors God as king draws also on other psalms (18; 50; 77) and Second Isaiah. The focus of this psalm and the verses selected for today is justice, which in the world of our ancestors in the faith was operative in the realm of patronage, a feature of fictive kinship. A patron is one with surplus who treats clients (needy people) as if they were family, hence, with favoritism. This is how the LORD treats his people (the just, the upright of heart), and all the people will witness this honorable behavior (God's glory). The birth of a savior is a gift beyond expectation. Truly such a patron outshines all others as the refrain reminds us.

* Nativity: Mass during the Day
Isaiah 52:7-10

Exile is a painful experience. The Polish experience is expressed in the poignant phrase: *żyć na wygnaniu,* "to live somewhere after one was chased out, driven out, banished, expatriated, without rights." The notion involves a sense of belonging and security which is shattered by forced ejection from a sacred place. Without diminishing the historical and cultural uniqueness of each case, perhaps only a person who has experienced an exile can appreciate its reversal.

Today Second Isaiah reports the joy of reversal of the Babylonia exile, but from a strange perspective. It is the watchmen, the ones who did not go into exile, who shout for joy. Scholars note that it was only the elite, the intelligentsia as it were, who were taken away. Ordinary folk remained. Yet both suffered. "How could we sing a song of the LORD / in a foreign land?" asked the deportees (Ps 137). Those who did not go into exile had no visionary leaders to lift their spirits or stir their hopes. The best news of all in the prophet's statement is that at last "all the ends of the earth" will see that God is worth believing in. God does care for and remember the people of divine concern. As this reading tells that the people saw God's redemption in progress, the gospel reading for today (John 1:1-18) speaks of Jesus as Word and light giving people the ability to see a new moment in God's redemptive will.

Responsorial Psalm: 98:1, 2-3, 5-6

Today's verses drawn from yet another psalm acclaiming God as king of the universe highlight a worldwide participation in the reign of God. Israel is saved, all the nations are witnesses, and the entire physical universe is transformed. Because the psalm borrows from the first reading ("all the ends of the earth," Ps 98:3; Isa 52:10), it is perfectly suited as a bridge to the gospel and as a link between all the cosmic references in the readings.

Sunday within the Octave of Christmas: The Holy Family of Jesus, Mary, and Joseph
Sirach 3:2-6, 12-14

While today's gospel (Matt 2:13-15, 19-23) highlights Joseph as a responsible husband and father, this first reading focuses on the obligations of sons. Honoring one's father means to submit to the father's will and to remain fiercely loyal to the patriarch. Such a son pleases God, who attends to the dutiful son's prayers. Whoever reveres his father will live a long life because the father will not have to kill the disobedient son as God requires (see Deut 21:18-21 about the glutton and drunkard; compare the opinion of people about Jesus in Matt 11:18-19). If one mirror-reads the concluding verses (12-14), that is, imagines the situation that it might plausibly be addressing, one might suspect that disrespect of fathers by sons did occur, perhaps often enough to warrant composition of these verses by the sage. Consider how Jacob at the instigation of his mother Rebecca treated his aged father, Isaac (Genesis 27). The prevailing motivation given by the sage for his advice is that God hears the prayers of a dutiful and honorable son. Considering the concern God shows toward Joseph in today's gospel, it is plausible to conclude that Joseph was an honorable son who revered his own father. When faced with challenges in his own married life, Joseph turned in prayer to God, who responded favorably as the gospel indicates.

Responsorial Psalm: 128:1-2, 3, 4-5

This psalm highlights the blessings that come to a person who fears the Lord. The word "fear" does not describe an emotion that causes trembling, the knees to weaken, and the like. It rather describes an awareness of who God is and how one relates to God. Acknowledging that the creature is not God will gain for the creature God's blessings in labor, in the family circle, and in all of Israel. In this case, the blessings are a fertile wife and many, presumably obedient, children.

or 1 Samuel 1:20-22, 24-28

The barren Hannah was the butt of abuse by Peninnah, a rival wife, who alone bore children to their husband, Elkanah. Hannah earnestly prayed in secret to the Lord for a son. No one knew what she prayed for: neither Elkanah, her husband, nor Eli, the priest who witnessed her prayer. The Lord heard Hannah's prayer. She conceived and bore a son. She named him Samuel, a name which means "name of God . . ." Because she promised it to the Lord when she requested a son, Hannah delivered Samuel to the sanctuary at Shilo probably some time after his third birthday, the customary age at which boys were weaned (see 2 Macc 7:27).

In Middle Eastern culture, a wife has little status in her husband's family until she bears a son. While this is a great blessing for the husband, it is also social security for the mother. The strongest emotional bond in the Middle East is between mother and [eldest] son. She will direct and control the son's life until she dies. In the light of this cultural information, a modern believer can understand Hannah's desperation: to give up a son, even to the Lord in fulfillment of a promise, is a heroic sacrifice. Nevertheless, each time Hannah went with Elkanah to offer sacrifice at the sanctuary, she brought Samuel a garment that she had made for him. Love yes, but also a measure of continuing maternal control. Eli the priest would bless Elkanah as he departed with his wife, "May the LORD repay you with children for the gift she has made to the LORD" (2:20). And indeed, God was not outdone by Hannah. She bore three sons and two daughters, while Samuel grew up in the service of the Lord.

The resonances of this story with Luke's report of Jesus being found in the Temple are somewhat evident. While Samuel stays in the sanctuary for life to serve the Lord, Jesus returns with his parents to Nazareth. Both serve the Lord but in different ways.

Responsorial Psalm: 84:2-3, 5-6, 9-10

Deeply moved by the sight of the Temple, a gifted pilgrim created this psalm to express his emotions. Yet is it not so much the dwelling place itself, or the Temple courts that stir the pilgrim. It is rather the realization that he is in the presence of the living God. The ancients knew that God actually resided in the sky, and ancient cultures believed that God was located directly above the deity's Temple on earth. The "hole in the sky" over this Temple gives one access to the realm of God. The sense of the presence of God is powerful in this place. Both Samuel and Jesus knew that, as did their parents. Periodic pilgrimages to God's house sharpens one's awareness of God's presence not just in the Temple, but everywhere in life.

* January 1 Octave Day of Christmas: Solemnity of the Blessed Virgin Mary, the Mother of God
Numbers 6:22-27

Many Christians recognize these verses as the Blessing of St. Francis written by him for Brother Leo, who requested a special, personal benediction. Others may recall that these verses form the traditional conclusion to the Synagogue Sabbath service. In the context of the Hebrew Bible, these verses emphasize the "face" of God and hearken back to the experience of Moses himself: "The LORD used to speak to Moses face to face, as one man speaks to another" (Exod 33:11). In this respect Moses was considered to be unique among all the prophets: "Since then no prophet has arisen in Israel like Moses, whom the LORD knew face to face" (Deut 34:10). But what of the persistent biblical tradition that no human being could survive such a face-to-face encounter with God: "But my face you cannot see, for no man sees me and still lives" (Exod 33:20)? The text does not say that such a vision is impossible, only that it can be fatal. That is why people who survive can express only awe and wonder. "I have seen God face to face . . . yet my life has been spared," marveled Jacob (Gen 32:31).

In Israel, the verses from Numbers had been used as a priestly blessing from very early times during the three feasts

(Passover, Pentecost, Tabernacles) when Israelites went to present themselves to the Lord to "see his face." Thus the phrase meant going on pilgrimage to the Temple in Jerusalem. The priestly verses, then, expressed the confident hope that those who came to experience God in the Temple would not be disappointed. The gospel (Luke 2:16-21) reports the responses of some who had met Jesus face to face: the shepherds went and told others; Mary pondered these things in her heart. How would you respond to a face-to-face meeting with God or the Risen Jesus?

Responsorial Psalm: 67:2-3, 5, 6, 8

Originally this psalm may have been a non-Israelite thanksgiving after a bountiful harvest. Appending the priestly prayer in the opening verses would have accommodated it to the Israelite tradition. When God displays the divine "face" (self), God manifests personal delight and gracious generosity. This is God's way of dealing with human beings (vv. 2-3). Nations should rejoice (vv. 5, 6) and so should all the earth (v. 8). God deals with human beings justly, as a father deals with family members. The final verse, "all the ends of the earth" (which has yielded its increase), is a fitting reference to Mary, since Jesus, the fruit of her womb, is part of this earth's "yield" (see Gal 4:4, which is the second reading for today; and relate also to today's gospel, Luke 2:41-52). These psalm verses make a fitting bridge between all three readings.

* Second Sunday after Christmas
Sirach 24:1-2, 8-12

Known as the "Praise of Wisdom," this poem (24:1-33) begins the second major division of Sirach (24–50). Today's verses are drawn from a twenty-two-line speech delivered by Wisdom in the first person (vv. 3-17, 19-22). The author introduces Wisdom in verses 1 and 2. By themselves, these verses do indeed indicate the honorable status of Wisdom, but both to modern and especially ancient ears, they are incomplete without verse 3. Modern listeners might repeat the folk-adage, "self-praise stinks." Ancient Mediterranean listeners would bristle to hear someone speak without humility, that is, without deliberately putting oneself down a notch or two so that others can raise one up to one's proper status. Verse 3 explains why the first two verses are culturally appropriate: Wisdom came from the mouth of the Most High. This explains the respect and reputation she enjoys in the assembly of the Most High, in the midst of her people, and in the multitude of the chosen.

Twenty-two lines imitate an acrostic poem, that is, one in which each line begins with a successive letter of the Hebrew alphabet. This speech is not an acrostic. The final verses of today's reading (8-12) tell us that God commanded Wisdom to dwell in Israel because she was unable to find a suitable place elsewhere on earth by a personal search. Dwelling in the "tent" is an allusion to the dwelling that God commanded Moses to build (Exod 25:8-19; 26:1-37). That she ministers there suggests that Wisdom as Law laid down the liturgical

rules to be followed in the worship of the Lord. She continued when the Temple replaced the tent, and she remains ever
present among God's people. Reference to Wisdom (spoken
by God) living in a tent (24:8) links nicely with the statement
in today's gospel that "God's word became human and [liter-
ally in Greek] pitched its tent among us" (John 1:14).

Responsorial Psalm: 147:12-13, 14-15, 19-20

These verses are drawn from the three quasi-independent
hymns that constitute this psalm: verses 1-6, 7-11, and 12-20,
which focus on God as Lord of Zion through the creative
word. Mention of Zion and repetition of various synonyms
for "word"–command, statutes, ordinances–demonstrate how
these verses serve as a suitable bridge between the first reading and the gospel. Indeed, the refrain makes that explicit:
"The Word of God became man and lived among us."

* January 6: Epiphany
Isaiah 60:1-6

Third Isaiah speaks a word of encouragement to the residents of Jerusalem. To offset the discouragement deriving from the trickle of returnees from exile, the prophet uses the "prophetic perfect" tense (v. 1: light has come, glory shines [has shone]), which firmly declares that salvation is still to come. An action initiated in the past is yet to be completed. Paltry beginnings should not discourage anyone. God lights up the Holy City, which invites all to gather and come (vv. 1-3). The imagery stirs hope. First the scattered deportees of Israel return ("your sons . . . and daughters"). Then come the non-Israelites from far away. "Riches of the sea" would indicate the region north to Tyre and Phoenicia; "Midian and Ephah" point to the region south to the Arabian desert and east to the Gulf of Aqabah; "Sheba" refers to south Arabia. Some scholars think Matthew in today's gospel (2:1-12) drew inspiration from these verses of Isaiah when he mentions gold and frankincense. The passage has long been associated with the feast of the Epiphany in the liturgy.

Responsorial Psalm: 72:1-2, 7-8, 10-11, 12-13

Traces of Isaiah 9:2-7 and 11:1-9 in this psalm support the opinion that it was composed in honor of King Hezekiah (715–687 B.C.E.) with verse 10 added still later (compare Isa 60:6-10). Today's verses praise the ideal kin-person's justice and judgment (1-2). He shall establish peace over the ideal expanse of Israel: from the Red Sea to the Mediterranean, from the desert to the Euphrates ("sea to sea," vv. 7-8). The psalmist pushes the boundaries even to Spain (Tarshish) and Ethiopia (Seba, vv. 10-11)! Why should this king's empire extend so far? Because he will vindicate the lowly, poor, and afflicted (vv. 12-13). Yes, as the refrain indicates, every nation can admire such a ruler.

* Baptism of the Lord (First Sunday in Ordinary Time)
Isaiah 42:1-4, 6-7

These verses are commonly identified as one of the four "Servant" Songs in Isaiah (42:1-4; 49:1-6; 50:4-9a; 52:13–53:12). Current scholarship suggests that they were an integral part of Second Isaiah (40–55) from the beginning and were not later additions. The Servant is Israel presented as a collectivistic individual. At the present time, approximately 80 percent of the world's population are collectivistic individuals. Such people stand in sharp contrast to individuals as they are known in Western cultures (representing just 20 percent of the world's population). Collectivistic personalities draw their identity from the group (nation, family) and do not want to stand out from the crowd. While earlier biblical scholarship talked about corporate personality, it is more appropriate today to speak of collectivistic personalities. Thus, while these Servant Songs in Isaiah sound as if they are describing a specific individual, they really describe the nation. Any individual member of this nation would readily identify with the description.

These particular verses deal with the destiny of the Servant. Above all, the Servant will reveal and establish justice or God's law to all the nations. The Servant will teach everything that is needed for leading a well-ordered life pleasing to God. Israel will not assume the posture of an arrogant and rushing victor, but will rather offer a living example of obedience to God's will. In this way will she be a light to the nations. One basic link between this reading and the gospel (Matt 3:13-17) is the notion of someone with whom God is pleased: the Servant and Jesus. What kind of job description would you write for such a person?

Responsorial Psalm: 29:1-2, 3-4, 3, 9-10

This hymn was borrowed from Canaanite culture where it was sung in honor of Baal, god of thunder and conqueror of the mighty waters. The Israelites substituted "voice of the LORD" for "voice of Baal" and repeated it seven times while singing this hymn in the liturgical assembly. Of course, thunder is the voice of the Lord, and these psalm verses point to today's Gospel reading in which the sky is torn open and the voice from the sky says of Jesus: "This is my beloved Son, with whom / I am well pleased."

or Isaiah 40:1-5, 9-11

These familiar verses report the commissioning of the prophet, Second Isaiah (author of Isaiah 40–55). Like all divine commissioning reports (e.g., Isaiah 6; Jeremiah 1), this one too takes place while the prophet is in an altered state of consciousness. In this state, the prophet has journeyed to the place where God dwells in the sky. He hears God address the assembly: "Comfort, give comfort to my people" (the imperatives are plural). God's message which the prophet hears and will in turn deliver to the people is that Jerusalem's, that is, the people's, guilt is expiated. To receive double from the Lord is not so much a description of quantity, or of the depths of God's anger, but rather that the purification process is now totally complete.

One of the heavenly council shouts out a further explanation of God's plan. God will personally lead a new Exodus along a new "way" (as early believers in Jesus described themselves, Acts 9:2; 19:9, 23). The "way" is a "way of life" that will please God (Isa 55:6-9).

The good news to be announced to the whole world from a high mountain is not so much a message as the continued existence of a people mercifully redeemed by their covenant God. Thus commissioned, Isaiah can begin his work as spokesperson for God, just as Jesus at his baptism is commissioned by God and confirmed in his identity: "You are my beloved Son; with you I am well pleased" (Luke 3:22).

Responsorial Psalm: 104:1b-2, 3-4, 24-25, 27-28, 29-30

This psalmist is incredibly "cultured," so to speak. His hymn echoes the Babylonian creation myth in which Marduk destroyed Tiamat (vv. 2-9), and seems familiar with the Hymn to the Sun by Amenhotep IV (vv. 19-26). Yet he is strongly rooted in his Israelite tradition. The Lord God magnificently and masterfully created the sky and the earth (vv. 1-4), the earth and sea, and the creatures that populate both (vv. 24-25). And all depend upon God who sustains them (vv. 27-30). This psalm's focus on an ever-caring God bridges well the commissioning stories of Second Isaiah and Jesus, each of whom signaled God's personal care for the people of the covenant.

Second Sunday in Ordinary Time
Isaiah 62:1-5

Disciples of Second Isaiah are quite likely the authors of Isaiah 56–66 some time after the completion of the second Temple, perhaps around 515 B.C.E. The prophet reports God's joyous announcement that a glorious new Zion will emerge now, secure from invasions but rather receiving recognition from other nations. Today's verses describe a new espousal of the once adulterous Israel (Hosea 1–2) with YHWH. Her new names are "My Delight" (Hephziba, 2 Kings 21:1) and "Espoused" *(be ʿula)*. The Hebrew for "espoused" derives from the word "ba'al," which can mean husband but was long associated with the deity of fertility cults. That God would use this name for reformed Israel testifies to the completeness and solidity of her conversion. No wonder that God the bridegroom rejoices in his bride, the people Israel. It is undoubtedly the image of bride that is intended to link this reading however superficially with the wedding at Cana (John 2) in today's gospel.

Responsorial Psalm: 96:1-2, 2-3, 7-8, 9-10

This enthronement psalm exhorts participants in Temple liturgy to put new meaning into familiar ritual ("sing . . . a new song," vv. 1-3). The next scene (vv. 7-10) is the open space in front of the gates to the Temple area. Just as royalty at their crowning or other festive occasions are greeted by visiting monarchs and dignitaries, so too should all the nations pay similar homage to God as King and acknowledge the divine rule. The final verse reflects the desire of Israel after centuries of foreign domination to experience the ultimate kingship of God who will govern people with equity and will render fair judgment to all.

Third Sunday in Ordinary Time
Nehemiah 8:2-4a, 5-6, 8-10

Nehemiah was a layperson appointed by the king to over-see the Restoration of Judah after the return from Babylonian Exile (537 B.C.E.). Ezra, the subject of today's verses, was a priest, indeed a scribe well versed in the Torah. He aimed to make that Torah the basic rule of life or, some would say, "the constitution" of this restored Theocracy. Scholars are not agreed on just how much of the Law (Torah) Ezra read, but it lasted about six or seven hours! The people listened atten-tively not because it was new but because it was their rule of life. On this occasion, Levites added instruction to the inter-pretation that Ezra gave.

The people's response involved three things. First, they said, "Amen, Amen," declaring their acceptance of what was read. Raising the hands was a gesture expressing need and depend-ence (see Ezra 9:5; Ps 28:2; 134:2), which God would ad-dress through the Torah being read. Prostration is of course an indication of humility, worship, and adoration. The exhor-tation by Ezra, Nehemiah, and the Levites that the people should not weep reveals yet another response to what was heard. The weeping was likely caused by the remorse which was stirred by a fresh hearing and interpretation of the Law. Ezra had a gift of making "ancient" laws relevant in striking new ways (see Ezra 9). As the people recognized the dimen-sions of their shortcomings and the seriousness of the com-mandments of God that they had disobeyed, they were understandably moved to tears.

These leaders, however, comforted and encouraged the people by saying: "Rejoicing in the LORD must be your strength [or protection]." On certain occasions, particularly liturgical celebrations, the recital of God's mighty deeds in the past prompted listeners to identify with and appropriate them in their present lives. God has always been good and gracious, a true cause for rejoicing. Such a joyous recollection would indeed provide strength or protection against divine judgment threatened against transgressors (e.g., Leviticus 26; Deuteronomy 27–28).

The final suggestion is to celebrate with a special meal featuring "rich foods" (literally "the fat pieces") and "sweet drinks" shared with those who had nothing prepared. Since such a meal could not be prepared spontaneously, it is plausible to conclude that this event was some sort of familiar ritual that was observed periodically. Participants all knew what to expect, and those that didn't could share in the preparations of those who did.

Some contemporary experts in targumic literature (targums are Aramaic paraphrases of the Hebrew Scriptures) suggest that Nehemiah 8, along with other passages in the Hebrew Bible, may have influenced the formation of synagogue services and its three-year Lectionary cycle (a reading from the Torah, from the Haphthorah = Prophets, and perhaps Psalms as a third reading).

Ezra read from the Torah outside the Temple walls. There was no accompanying sacrifice. The entire event leaves the impression that the Torah is greater than the Temple and its sacrifices. This would be quite a stunning thought to the people. (Could it be another reason why they wept?) This selection from Nehemiah is linked to the gospel (Luke 1:1-4; 4:14-21) by the fact that Scripture is read and interpreted (by Ezra; by Jesus) with startling results in each case.

Responsorial Psalm: 19:8, 9, 10, 15

Verses 8-15 were perhaps originally an independent psalm hymning YHWH's revelation in the Law. YHWH's name (LORD in English translations) appears seven times, the number of perfection. No wonder the first verse we read is: "the law of the LORD is perfect." There are also different words for "Law": law, decrees, precepts, command, ordinances, and words. There are a variety of descriptors: perfect, trustworthy, right, clear, true, just, spirit, and life. The effect of observing the Law is all-encompassing: refreshes the soul, gives wisdom to the simple, rejoices the heart, enlightens the eye. The conclusion is a classic prayer seeking to find favor with God, rock and redeemer. Truly Ezra and Jesus sought to teach the life-giving aspects of God's law whose riches are captured in this brief but brilliant psalm.

Fourth Sunday in Ordinary Time
Jeremiah 1:4-5, 17-19

God communicates with human beings in altered states of consciousness. In his experience of being called by God (627–626 B.C.E.), Jeremiah carries on a dialogue which is not reported today (vv. 6-8). We hear only what God said to Jeremiah to open the dialogue. Mainly God says that even before Jeremiah's conception God designed a plan for him. Essentially, God intended to have a strong, intimate relationship with Jeremiah. A key characteristic of holy men (which includes prophets) in all cultures is having experiential contact with the spirit world; in Jeremiah's case the spirit is God ("I knew you"). By dedicating Jeremiah, God set him apart for a special service, namely to be God's spokesperson to Judah and the nations with which its political life was entangled. The message is a call to national reform, an exhortation to return to complete fidelity to God.

The essence of verses 17-19 is to warn Jeremiah that his forty-year ministry will not be easy. His audience, Judah's kings and princes, priests and people, will vehemently and violently resist. Jeremiah should not lose heart ("be not crushed") because God will strengthen him for the task. The prophet's enemies will not prevail over him. The obvious link with today's gospel (Luke 4:21-30) is explicit in Jesus' statement to his neighbors: "no prophet is accepted in his own native place." God's protection was evident in Jesus being able to escape the furious mob safely, just as Jeremiah escaped many trying situations in his career.

Responsorial Psalm: 71:1-2, 3-4, 5-6, 15, 17

Just as Jeremiah's report of his call experience reflects elements and vocabulary of previous call narratives (Moses, Gideon), so does the prayer for deliverance by this old man reflect and drawn upon vocabulary of similar psalms of lament. Lifelong dependence upon and confidence in God (v. 6) forms a plausible bridge between the reading from Jeremiah and today's gospel.

Fifth Sunday in Ordinary Time
Isaiah 6:1-2a, 3-8

In 742 B.C.E., Isaiah was in the Temple when he received his call from God to be a prophet. God called Isaiah in an altered state of consciousness experience, the customary way in which God communicates with human beings (see 1 Sam 3:1). The circumstances were ideal for such an encounter. The fragrance of burning coals, incense (smoke), and burnt offerings, all capable of inducing a religious ecstatic trance, filled the Temple. The seraphim, an adjective meaning fiery but used in this passage as a noun, refers to members of YHWH's court in the sky. This image could have been prompted by the burning coals but was interpreted by the visionary according to imagery available in his tradition. The sound track of the vision ("Holy, holy, holy," etc.) was quite likely inspired and initiated by the Temple liturgy. In this vision, YHWH commissions and empowers Isaiah to be a spokesperson for the divine message to his contemporaries. Isaiah, who at first feels unworthy, is emboldened by this experience to accept. "Here I am, send me." The link between this reading and Jesus' call of his first followers in the gospel (Luke 5:1-11) is obvious, though their call is perhaps not as dramatic as Isaiah's.

Responsorial Psalm: 138:1-2, 2-3, 4-5, 7-8

In this psalm of praise, the author expresses indebtedness to God for assistance in distress. The debt is paid to God by broadcasting God's beneficence to all the kings of the earth who join in the hymn of praise. God's steadfast loving kindness toward human beings endures forever.

Sixth Sunday in Ordinary Time
Jeremiah 17:5-8

These verses have a clear echo in Psalm 1 (today's responsorial psalm), but the ideas are common and widespread in
the ancient world. The person who trusts in the LORD is con-
trasted with one who trusts only in fellow human beings. The
contrast is expressed by an image drawn from nature: a barren bush (one who trusts in human beings) growing (?) in an
inhospitable environment is not like a tree (one who trusts in
the LORD) planted near a stream. The choice of the phrase
"lava waste" (v. 6, the inhospitable environment in which the
barren bush grows) to translate a phrase more commonly
rendered "parched places" (of the desert) stirs interest. Lava
turns to rock when it cools; lahar, the mudflow down the side
of a volcano, eventually dries and turns into a grayish dust.
Bricks and the like can be made from it, but it doesn't support vegetation at first. Yet, a shoot might do better in lahar,
at least for a while, than in lava. One wonders whence in ancient Palestine the imagery was derived. (Berekhat Ram near
Mount Hermon is an extinct volcano.) On the other hand,
"salt and empty earth" is a common description of desert
wasteland in the Bible (Deut 29:23; Ps 107:34; Job 39:6;
Zeph 2:9). The imagery is well chosen even if the inspiration
remains a puzzle. In today's gospel (Luke 6:17, 20-26), Jesus
uses makarisms to describe a person who trusts in God and
woes to describe those who trust only in themselves.

Responsorial Psalm: 1:1-2, 3, 4 and 6

This psalm, which echoes the verses in Jeremiah, makes a good bridge between that reading and the gospel. Blessed indeed are they who hope in the LORD rather than in other human beings.

Seventh Sunday
in Ordinary Time
1 Samuel 26:2, 7-9, 12-13, 22-23

This impressive story is told more than once in the Bible. This version derives from the Early Source (King Solomon's time), thus presenting David as a very human person who is capable of noble and shameful deeds. In this case, he does a very noble thing. Saul seeks David's life and pursues him with three thousand men to the desert of Ziph just west of the Dead Sea. David's men number just six hundred. David and his nephew Abishai (1 Chron 2:16) sneak into Saul's camp and come upon Saul asleep. Abishai seeks David's permission to kill Saul, proposing that God has personally delivered the enemy into David's hand. David refuses to harm the Lord's anointed, but takes Saul's spear and water jug as they flee the camp. From the opposite slope David informs Saul's troops of his virtue. He has demonstrated his respect for Saul, his enemy but the Lord's anointed, by sparing his life. David's motivation is his conviction that the Lord will reward "justice and faithfulness," which is what David's behavior in this instance manifests. Both of those words in the Mediterranean cultural value system mean "enduring loyalty to one's kin," or loyalty to the kinsmen no matter what. (David was married to Saul's daughter, Michal: 1 Sam 18:20-21.) The link that binds this reading with today's gospel (Luke 6:27-38) is quite likely Jesus' command to love one's enemies and do good to them. Jesus' exhortation goes beyond the kinship obligations which guided David's noble behavior.

Responsorial Psalm: 103:1-2, 3-4, 8, 10, 12-13

The refrain rephrases verse 8: merciful and gracious is the Lord. The Hebrew word for merciful relates to the womb and suggests a sentiment deeper than the word "gracious." In this hymn of praise, a person rescued from illness recognizes God's favor not only in restored health but also in compassionate forgiveness. These sentiments form a beautiful bridge between the first reading and today's gospel.

Eighth Sunday in Ordinary Time
Sirach 27:4-7

The link between this reading and the gospel (Luke 6:39-45) is probably human speech (v. 45). Sirach's point is that a person's speech reveals much about him. In a culture which is not only nonintrospective but antiintrospective (1 Sam 16:7), external characteristics such as one's speech are the basis for judging others. The Greek word translated "husks" is literally "dunghill, dung, refuse." The image is jarring: a person's filth becomes obvious from what that person says. The other images are more congenial. Just as a potter tests his handiwork in the oven, so do listeners "test" others by their conversation. And just as the fruit of a tree indicates how well it has been cultivated, so too does human speech reveal whether a person is cultivated, well trained, finely disciplined. The conclusion (v. 7) is obvious: withhold judging others until they have spoken, and their speech has been evaluated.

Responsorial Psalm: 92:2-3, 13-14, 15-16

Returning to a consideration that is repeated in a few psalms, this psalmist also describes and praises the just person. Such a one flourishes in intimate relationship with God, in the very dwelling place of God. Such a one remains loyal for life, and well into old age will declare God's justice. The speech of this just person, so beautifully described by the psalmist, serves to link the first reading with today's gospel.

Ninth Sunday in Ordinary Time
1 Kings 8:41-43

The major portion of Solomon's speech at the dedication of the Temple (vv. 31-53) asks YHWH to attend to prayers offered in (or directed toward) the Temple. Today's verses (41-43) concern the prayer of a foreign pilgrim, one of seven examples given by Solomon. One might wonder why a foreigner would journey to Jerusalem to pray to a god that is not his own. Ancient peoples (including Israel, as the biblical record indicates) inclined toward polytheism (or in Israel's case, henotheism). It was worth the effort to intercede with a deity whose reputation for effective responses was known far and wide. Solomon cleverly reminds God that if a foreigner's request is heard and completely fulfilled, it will only redound to God's honor and reputation. Since all God-talk is rooted in human experience as culturally conditioned, the Middle Eastern monarch Solomon, who was concerned about his honor and reputation, exhibits a similar concern about God's honor and reputation, especially among foreigners. The link to the gospel (Luke 7:1-10) in which a foreigner confidently brings a request to Jesus is clear.

Responsorial Psalm: 117:1, 2

The sentiments of this shortest of all psalms in the Bible is rather surprising. Foreign nations are invited to praise the God of Israel for the Lord's steadfast loving kindness toward the Israelites ("us")! Even if these nations did not become followers of Israel's God, admiring that deity's benevolence

41

to the people chosen is admirable and perhaps enviable. The psalmist may have seen it as a first step in the right direction. The brief verses link the readings well.

Tenth Sunday in Ordinary Time
1 Kings 17:17-24

The similarity between this story about Elijah and the widow's son in Sidon and Jesus and the widow's son in Nain is obvious. One cultural element binds them together: a widow's loss of a son. In the Middle East, though the customary marriage partner is a patrilateral parallel cousin ("father's brother's daughter"), that woman is never fully included in her husband's family unless and until she bears a son. The life-long emotional bond that develops between mother and son is one of the strongest in this culture. The son is more important to her than her husband (see 1 Sam 1:8). Now that the widows in these stories are bereft of husband and of son, the only significant men that might be left is their respective fathers. If the father is dead, the widow is in a very difficult situation. This helps appreciate the gift Elijah bestowed on this widow.

A second question of interest to modern readers is: How did Elijah restore this boy to life? Researchers inclined toward a scientific biomedical perspective point out that there is insufficient medical data in this report (as well as in the gospel) to definitively declare the boy was dead. He may have been comatose or in another condition. These same researchers hasten to add that it is similarly impossible to deny that he was indeed dead! In the estimation of the ancients who reported these stories, the dead person was indeed dead (whatever that meant to them).

Biblical scholars highlight what the tradition emphasizes. Elijah was a "man of God" (vv. 18, 24), as was Jesus (Luke 4:34, "holy one of God"). These biblical phrases describe a "holy man/holy woman," a figure common in many cultures. Further, cultures that recognize a holy person describe that person as having direct access to the deity. This person's primary function is to heal. Whether by means of prayer or sympathetic magic, Elijah performs his function as a holy man of God. He stirs God to restore breath to the child. Jesus does the same for the widow of Nain. The people's response is also similar. The widow acknowledges Elijah as a man of God who speaks God's word; the people identify Jesus as prophet through whom God visits them.

Responsorial Psalm: 30:2, 4, 5-6, 11, 12, 13

The psalmist's hymns have sentiments of indebtedness to God for rescuing him from a near death situation (the nether world; the pit; converted mourning into dancing). Perhaps only one who has shared this experience can appreciate it. The verses form a most appropriate bridge between today's similar readings.

First Sunday of Lent
Deuteronomy 26:4-10

The principle guiding the selection of readings from the Old Testament during Lent is that each presents some information about the history of salvation. The second reading (from the apostles) was selected to suit the gospel and first reading, perhaps even forming a bridge between them. The "creed" at the center of today's reading (vv. 5-9) formerly had been considered as the oldest Israelite creed perhaps originating at Gilgal, but this view is now widely abandoned. The creed is indeed old and may have borrowed from the cult, but its pattern is typical of the Deuteronomist. Oppression (v. 6), cry for help (v. 7), and God's favorable and effective response (v. 8) are found elsewhere too (e.g., Judg 3:7-11). The father in this creed is Jacob, also known as Israel (Gen 35:10). The switch to the plural in verse 6 is typical of people with collectivistic personalities, who draw their identity from a group. What sounds like a very individualistic statement (my father) is actually collectivistic as the subsequent plurals indicate. The gifts offered to God express Israel's indebtedness to the One who redeemed them from Egypt and continues to rescue them from threatening situations.

Responsorial Psalm: 91:1-2, 10-11, 12-13, 14-15

This psalm welcomes a pilgrim to the Temple. Ritually, the pilgrim pronounced the sentiment in verse 2, and the priest offered assurance of God's blessings here, on the return journey home, and indeed throughout life (vv. 10-11, 12-13). The concluding verses (14-15) are an oracle spoken by the priest in God's name. Because verse 12 is reported in the gospel (Luke 4:1-13), this psalm constitutes a perfect link to it.

Second Sunday of Lent
Genesis 15:5-12, 17-18

In a trance, an altered state of consciousness (vv. 1 and 12), Abraham receives God's promise of an heir (v. 5, fully explained in vv. 2-4) and of "this land" (vv. 7-12). Abraham asks for a sign, which would also be a guarantee of the promises. Walking between split animals (which God does symbolically in the "smoking fire pot and a flaming torch") indicates a willingness to accept this violent fate if one does not keep one's covenant promise. The extent of "this land" (from Wadi el-Arish in Egypt to the Euphrates) reflects the greatest extent of the land in the time of David. Since these verses derive from both the J and E traditions (950 and 850 B.C.E. respectively), it is clear that this event situated in Abraham's lifetime (around 1800 B.C.E.) has been heavily edited. Some modern scholars propose that many of these pentateuchal traditions actually were formulated in the Persian period to suit the historical context of that time, namely Judah as a Persian satrapy. As Christians reflect on these episodes in the history of salvation reported in the lenten liturgy, it is well to recall the development of beliefs that is common to all human beings. One link between this reading and the gospel (Luke 9:28b-36) is God's communication with human beings in altered states of consciousness.

Responsorial Psalm: 27:1, 7-8, 8-9, 13-14

The references in this psalm to seeing the face of God have two meanings. One, it is a common way to refer to a visit to the Temple. Two, it also refers to experiences of God in altered states of consciousness, very common in this culture as the many biblical references to this experience from Genesis to Revelation make evident. The psalmist yearns for God to rescue him from a difficult situation as he yearns to experience God more intimately. The concluding verse (14) is a word of encouragement spoken by the priest. Be patient, wait for the Lord. As the first reading and the gospel make clear, when the time is right, God visits faithful believers.

Third Sunday of Lent
Exodus 3:1-8a, 13-15

By killing the firstborn and enslaving the Israelites, Pharaoh was thwarting God's promises to Abraham (progeny and land). In an altered state of consciousness experience (fire flaming out of a bush but not consuming it), Moses encounters God personally who commissions him to lead the people out of bondage. Moses exercises proper cultural humility (v. 11) and offers God still three more opportunities to assure him. In today's reading, Moses asks a very "personal" question; he seeks to learn God's name, since "God of your fathers" (literally: "God of your father," v. 6) is no longer adequate. To know another's name is to become capable of controlling that person. Some scholars think that explains God's somewhat cryptic answer. It is not so much a name as a function: "I am who am," or "I AM," which is in a Hebrew causative tense best translated as "the One who creates or causes things to exist." The actual name, YHWH, is the third person singular of the verb in question. God will see to the fulfillment of the promises made to Abraham.

Responsorial Psalm: 103:1-2, 3-4, 6-7, 8, 11

Quite likely mention of God making known his ways to Moses in verse 7 inspired the selection of this optimistic psalm of praise as a response to the first reading. The word "kind/kindness" repeated so often in these verses translates a Hebrew word which means "steadfast loving kindness," a sentiment or value that is shared only among kin. When God declares that this is a divine trait, it strains credulity and heightens the sense of indebtedness. What other response could they make for rescue from the Egyptians and the gift of a land flowing with milk and honey?

Fourth Sunday of Lent
Joshua 5:9a, 10-12

This is the third of six "official" Passover festivals mentioned in the Old Testament. It is the first Passover celebrated by the community in Canaan at the end of the forty-year-long journey through the wilderness. In this instance it does not seem to be a "family" celebration. No mention of lamb on this occasion suggests that this is actually the older festival of Unleavened Bread (Exod 23:15; 34:18) to which the sacrifice of lamb was added at a later time. When both feasts were united, the Passover was celebrated on the fourteenth and the Unleavened bread on the fifteenth of Nisan.

Since they just entered the land, where did they obtain grain? Scholars say they brought the grain with them; others say Canaanites celebrating their harvest festival shared it with them, gave it to them, while still others say they simply took it. The important thing is that they had the wherewithal to celebrate an important feast. Perhaps even more important is the cessation of the manna indicating that the period of Moses and the wandering is now officially closed.

There is a cultural point that should be noted. God's statement of having "removed the reproach of Egypt [shame] from you [Israel]" (v. 9a) is vital in this text-segment. In a way, it explains why the feast was shared in communal fashion. Being slaves in Egypt humiliated Israel and Israel's God in the eyes of other nations who scoffed at them and their God (see Zeph 2:8-9). As God said of the Exodus: "I . . . freed you from their slavery, breaking the yoke they had laid upon you and letting you walk erect" (Lev 26:13). Now they celebrate their freedom with this festival meal.

Responsorial Psalm: 34:2-3, 4-5, 6-7

The verses selected from this alphabetical psalm for today's response sing of God's care for those who seek the Lord. Echoing God's action of removing Israel's shame mentioned in the first reading, the composer of verses 6-7 notes that the one who turns to the Lord in a time of need will not be ignored and will not have to "blush with shame."

Fifth Sunday of Lent
Isaiah 43:16-21

In another of his poetic masterpieces, Second Isaiah presents imagery depicting the Exodus from Egypt, only to caution his audience about glorying so much in the past that they fail to perceive what God is doing in their present (vv. 18-19). "Do you not perceive it?" These words are addressed to exiles in Babylon who understandably might not be as perceptive as the prophet who sees and proclaims hope of restoration in a difficult situation. The final line reminds them that God expects praise for divine benevolence.

Responsorial Psalm: 126:1-2, 2-3, 4-5, 6

The creative psalmist composed a stirring poem to envelop the lament and petition in verses 4-5 ("restore our fortunes . . ."). The prevailing imagery is of people returning from exile, rejoicing, laughing, shouting for joy. The return to Judah, however, was met by resistance and hostility from the local population. This is very likely the context for this psalm, hence the lament and prayer. The psalm enjoyed popularity and long life as a song which was sung during each pilgrimage to the holy city.

* Palm Sunday
of the Lord's Passion[1]
Isaiah 50:4-7

Just like the other Servant Songs, this third in the series of
four from Second Isaiah describes the nation Israel in history
and in captivity. She will recognize herself in the persecuted,
suffering, sick person, just as Isaiah (1:4, 6) described: "Ah,
sinful nation, people laden with wickedness. / . . . From the
sole of the foot to the head / there is no sound spot." The very
last verses of today's text-segment are especially noteworthy.
The Lord God is my help; I am not disgraced. The apparently
shameful appearance and behavior of this servant is not really
shameful if God is on his side. It is important for a male to
defend his honor at all costs. But if a male finds himself in a
losing situation such as being forced to go to court, which is
a definite no-win situation, then the male's honorable behavior is to endure the worst without flinching or crying. The
honorable aspect of what seems to be shameful behavior, of
course, is the notion that Mark's Passion story in its entirety
(Palm Sunday and Easter Vigil Gospel reading together)
fleshes out for Jesus. While Jesus seemed to be irredeemably
shamed in the betrayal, trial, crucifixion, death, and burial in
a stranger's tomb, God raised him from the dead. God must
have been very pleased with Jesus to honor him in this way.

[1] For commentary on the Old Testament readings of the Triduum, see
John J. Pilch, *The Triduum and Easter Sunday: Breaking Open the Scripture* (Collegeville: The Liturgical Press, 2000).

Responsorial Psalm: 22:8-9, 17-18, 19-20, 23-24

This lament of a person who suffers unjustly but patiently is quoted thirteen times in the New Testament and nine times alone in the Passion story. The psalmist is not complaining, shows no bitterness, makes no allusion to sin, does not declare personal innocence, and makes no defense against unjust charges. The suffering petitioner simply places himself entirely in the hands of God. In this he finds great peace.

The first segment (vv. 8-9) reports the shameful taunts, the inhuman ridicule. The next segment literally claims that persecutors have mauled his hands and feet as would a lion (vv. 17-18). The petitioner beseeches God to hear his prayer (vv. 19-20). The final segment that announces a public thanksgiving in the assembly testifies to the fact that God came to the rescue (vv. 23-24).

* Easter Sunday
Acts 10:34a, 37-43

To appreciate the readings of Easter time, it is helpful to understand a common human experience known as altered states of consciousness that are different from "normal" or "ordinary" consciousness. Brain and nervous system research indicates all human beings are capable of such experiences. Indeed, many are familiar with daydreaming, road trance (hypnosis while driving, yet obeying all laws and arriving at one's destination safely, etc.), and similar altered states. Cultures give distinctive interpretations to such experiences, but some cultures are reluctant to acknowledge them as healthy elements of human experience. Psychiatric research indicates that in some cultures, people can expect to see their deceased loves ones in an altered state of consciousness for as long as five years after the death, and sometimes longer. Anthropological studies recount that altered states of consciousness experiences are common in the circum-Mediterranean world of the present and of the past.

Peter delivers his speech within the context of his experience with Cornelius, a centurion of the Italian Cohort (Acts 10:1–11:18). In ecstatic trance, Cornelius is instructed to seek out Peter. Peter, also in ecstatic trance, is instructed by God that all foods are clean. When Cornelius personally repeats his experience to Peter, Peter makes a speech, some verses of which have been selected for today's reading.

Of interest to our reflection is Peter's report about experiencing the Risen Jesus. Peter notes that "God . . . granted that he be visible, not to all the people, but to us." Of course,

56

God is the one who "hard-wired" human beings with the capacity for varieties of consciousness, and God can also select the subjects of specific experiences. Sometimes God can even communicate with "enemies" in an altered state of consciousness (e.g., Nebuchadnezzar in Daniel 2). While all human beings are indeed capable of the experience, the experiences will always be individual and culture specific.

Peter also observes that they ate and drank with the risen Jesus. This is not a literary device but rather the report of an actual experience. The Israelite tradition believed that holy men *(ṣaddiq, ḥasid)* would eat at three-legged golden tables overflowing with delicacies in "the world to come." In the Israelite tradition, the phrase "the world to come" points to that place where the righteous will go after they die and depart from "this world." Psychological anthropologists would call that world "alternate reality," in contrast to this world which is ordinary reality, or culturally consensual reality. Thus some experiences in altered states of consciousness are experiences of alternate reality, including "the world to come," which is parallel to ordinary or consensual reality, or as the Israelite tradition calls it "this world."

Finally, Peter reports the consequences of seeing the Risen Jesus in an altered state of consciousness. The apostles were commissioned to preach and testify to Jesus as appointed by God to judge the living and the dead. Anthropologists observed that two common results of alternate states of consciousness experiences are that the visionary (1) finds a solution to a problem, or (2) is strengthened to embark on a new path in life. Clearly Peter and the apostles experienced the second effect. This reading from Acts relates well with the gospel (John 20:1-9) in which Mary of Magdala, Simon Peter, and the other disciple find the empty tomb but do not yet experience the Risen Jesus. It is the normal, first stage of experience after the death of a loved one.

Responsorial Psalm: 118:1-2, 16-17, 22-23

This is an entrance psalm from a Temple liturgy perhaps at a "Gate of Righteousness" which is offering solemn praise to

God. The psalm also appears to have been associated with pilgrimages to Jerusalem on the Feast of Tabernacles. It was an integral part of the Passover celebration recited in conjunction with filling the fourth cup of wine. The first two verses initiate the communal expression of indebtedness. Verses 16-17 echo Moses' song in Exodus 15, while the final verses (22-23) are quite likely an ancient proverb highlighting the difference that faith or loyalty can make. One person's junk becomes another person's treasure by faith. The late Fr. Carroll Stuhlmueller suggested that the psalm refrain (v. 24) "this is the day the LORD has made" is better translated "on the day when the Lord takes action." Indeed, on that day, Jesus was raised from the dead.

Second Sunday of Easter
Acts 5:12-16

For the Sundays of Easter in each year the first reading is taken from Acts of the Apostles in parallel and progressive selections: the life of the early Church, its witness, and its growth.

Today's reading is clearly about its phenomenal growth and the increasing success of the apostles in healing many sick people. The activity is centered in Solomon's Portico at the eastern end of the Temple, but it also extends into the "streets." The Greek word here is the same Jesus used in the parable about a man whose invitations to dinner were spurned: "Go out quickly into the streets and alleys of the town and bring in here the poor and crippled, the blind and the lame" (Luke 14:21). The benevolence of God extends beyond the Temple and aids the poor and needy wherever they may be. While the Jesus movement has not yet moved outside of Jerusalem, people who live in nearby towns come into the holy city in search of healing. All obtained the healing they sought.

The sick who sought at the very least to encounter Peter's healing shadow were similar to the hemorrhaging woman who only sought to touch the fringe of Jesus' garment (Luke 8:44). Medical anthropologists and even scientists investigating alternative therapies understand and readily admit many yet unresolved mysteries in human healing. The human will to health is powerful and not completely understood. While this report gives no specifics except to note that some were disturbed by unclean spirits, the sick people experienced real and significant changes in their conditions.

Responsorial Psalm: 118:2-4, 13-15, 22-24

This is a psalm traditionally identified as a "thanksgiving," but in view of the fact that "thank you" in the Middle East terminates a relationship, it is more appropriately termed a psalm of praise or a psalm of indebtedness. Gratitude in the Middle East and in other cultures expresses a sense of being in another's debt for the kindness or favor experienced. Verses 13-15 are the sentiments of a collectivistic individual who is grateful for the Lord's intervention. Verses 22-23 are cited in different contexts in the New Testament. Peter drew on it in his preaching (Acts 4:11) relating it to God raising Jesus from the dead after being "rejected" like the faithful Servant of Isaiah (53:3: "spurned"). Redemption wrought by God through Jesus has put all in God's debt.

Third Sunday of Easter
Acts 5:27-32, 40b-41

The note on which today's reading ends, namely, that the apostles gladly suffer dishonor because of preaching Jesus, actually permeates the entire selection. Having been freed from prison by an angel (Acts 5:23), the apostles are again apprehended and brought before the Sanhedrin. The high priest accuses them of trying to shame him and the Sanhedrin for the death of Jesus. The apostles reply by confirming that. They associate Roman crucifixion (how Jesus died) with the Hebraic form of capital punishment when they state "you had him killed by hanging him on a tree" (Acts 5:30; see Deut 21:22-23; Josh 8:29; 10:26-27). God's curse rests on one who dies in this manner.

The apostles report the great insight which they reached on the basis of their experience of the Risen Jesus in altered states of consciousness experiences. Since only God could raise a person from the dead, and they have experienced the Risen Jesus alive, then quite obviously God was pleased with Jesus despite his shameful death. God exalted him. Instead of exploring this further, the Sanhedrin forbid them from speaking further about Jesus and dismissed them. The final sentence of today's selection very likely refers to the flogging (dishonor) that the apostles received but which was omitted in today's selection (40a). It is also curious that verse 42 was not included: "they [the apostles] did not stop teaching and proclaiming the Messiah, Jesus."

Responsorial Psalm: 30:2, 4, 5-6, 11-12, 13

These selected sentiments of gratitude from someone who was rescued, perhaps even quite suddenly, from sickness (v. 4) fit the first reading quite well. "You changed my mourning into dancing" (v. 13) can be associated with the apostles' conviction that to suffer dishonor for preaching about Jesus is actually honorable for them in the eyes of God, the only arbiter of true honor. Small wonder the composer invites all to join in expressing his enormous debt to God his benefactor.

Fourth Sunday of Easter
Acts 13:14, 43-52

Continuing the theme of the growth of the early community of believers, today's crafted verses (which omit John Mark's separation from Paul [Acts 13:13], which may have been prompted by unresolved conflict between them) describe the mixed response to Paul and Barnabas' preaching activity in Pisidian Antioch. The crowd in the synagogue responds enthusiastically: many (v. 43) and later the whole city came (v. 44) out to hear them. Many followed them like disciples (v. 43; compare Luke 5:11, 27-28; 9:11, 23, 57-61; 18:22, 28, 43). Since the reputation (honor) of these two increases, that of the local Judeans diminishes. Honor or reputation or fame is a limited commodity in this culture. If one gains, another loses. To cut them off at the knees, the local Judeans contradict what Paul says, "blaspheming" or "slandering" him (the literal meaning of the Greek text).

The words put into the mouths of Paul and Barnabas by Luke as a response to their opponents need to be properly understood. Some scholars argue that Paul's statements in his letters can be read as indicating his mission was to diaspora Judeans living among Gentiles (rather than to Gentiles pure and simple), while Peter and companions ministered to Judeans in Palestine. "We now turn to the Gentiles" is better translated "we now turn to the Israelites living among the Gentiles." As Paul himself has noted, Gentiles entering the predominantly Israelite Jesus groups do so "contrary to nature" (Rom 11:24). In actual fact, only a small number of such

Gentiles will be allowed to enter (Rom 11:25). Those Gentiles who were delighted to hear what Paul said (Acts 13:48) were not Gentile pure and simple (as the dichotomy Judean and Gentile are customarily translated), but rather Gentiles already on the Israelite side, god-fearers (e.g., Ethiopian eunuch, Acts 8:26ff.; Tabitha, Acts 9:36ff.; Cornelius, Acts 10; and Sergius Publius, Acts 13:7ff.). Finally, unlike elsewhere, the elite women adherents to local Judean customs and the heads of the city are used as leverage to kick Paul and Barnabas out. For such people, Paul and Barnabas pose a threat to social order. The community of believers does indeed grow, but in a different way than we have customarily thought. The symbolic gesture of Paul and Barnabas (shaking dust from the feet) is quite appropriate because it is precisely the response that Jesus proposed for the "lost sheep of the house of Israel" (Matt 10:14) who would not accept the disciples' preaching.

Responsorial Psalm: 100:1-2, 3, 5

As the respected late Old Testament scholar Fr. Carroll Stuhlmueller reminded his readers, the Hebrew word in verse 1 is in the singular: "land." The reference is only to the house of Israel. Verse 3, well translated here, makes that quite clear: "his we are; his people, the flock he tends," a sentiment taken up in the refrain. It is healthy for modern believers to recognize and acknowledge accommodation of biblical texts in the liturgy, a practice which this response admirably illustrates. As non-Israelite worshipers, modern believers should be aware of this accommodation too often taken for granted.

Fifth Sunday of Easter
Acts 14:21-27

Paul and Barnabas now visit the communities which were established on the first journey. The visits feature two elements: a message about participation in the kingdom of God and the appointment of local leaders. The message is: "It is necessary for us to undergo many hardships to enter the kingdom of God" (v. 22). The word "necessary" has already been associated with Jesus Messiah who "had to suffer" before rising from the dead (Luke 24:46-47, translated differently in the NAB). Paul too "had to suffer" much in preaching the Lord in his ministry (Acts 9:15-16). Now for the first time in Acts all believers "have to suffer" in solidarity with Messiah Jesus and his ministers in order to enter the kingdom. This simply echoes Jesus' earlier exhortation to deny self, take up one's cross, and follow him (Luke 9:23-27).

They also appointed "elders" (v. 23) in each community. This is the same word that Luke-Acts uses exclusively to designate Judean authorities, particularly rulers of the Jerusalem Council (along with chief priests and scribes: Luke 9:22; 20:1; 22:52; Acts 4:5, 8, 23; 6:12). Clearly, the majority membership of these communities is of the house of Israel who have embraced Jesus as Messiah. The community continues to grow.

Responsorial Psalm: 145:8-9, 10-11, 12-13

According to the Babylonian Talmud (Ber. 4b), whoever recited this psalm three times a day (as it is in the synagogues) would certainly find a place in the world to come.

The sentiments are a suitable response to the first reading, which tells believers in Messiah Jesus how they might gain their place in the kingdom. The principal theme of the psalm is praise and there are references to growing inclusiveness: The Lord is good to all; toward all his works. The kingdom is for all ages, and God's dominion endures through all generations.

Sixth Sunday of Easter
Acts 15:1-2, 22-29

Christian Pharisees express concern that those who join the Judaic Messianist group should also accept the traditional marks of Judaic identity, such as circumcision and dietary laws. These critics do not doubt the faith of the newcomers, but they view the boundaries of the kingdom of God as identical with the boundaries of Israel. They object to Paul's acceptance of uncircumcised Gentile god-fearers for whom he also suspends the kosher laws. In contrast, the Christian Pharisees continue to observe all the purity rules and embrace Jesus as Messiah as well.

The discussion at Jerusalem results in a decision recorded in writing and delivered by Paul and Barnabas to that minority of believers of Gentile origin residing in Antioch, Syria, and Cilicia. Essentially, the decision proscribes four things in the order discussed in Leviticus 17–18: meat sacrificed to idols and thus contaminated; blood; anything that has been strangled; and illicit sexual relations (NAB translates this "unlawful marriage"). It is likely that blood and strangled meat refer to the same thing, namely, a slaughtered animal from whom the blood was not completely drained. The judgment thus pertains to social order more than to Judaic identity. Its purpose is to maintain harmonious relationships between the majority Judaic members and the minority Gentile members in mixed congregations.

Responsorial Psalm: 67:2-3, 5, 6, 8

Today's verses resonate with a certain "universalistic" note: nations, peoples, all the ends of the earth. The verse omitted (7) gives the reason for these sentiments, namely, a bountiful harvest. Israel perceived God's activity across the world chiefly in rain and fertility and sometimes international politics. Nonetheless, the refrain captures the main idea: "Let all the nations praise you!"

* The Ascension of the Lord
Acts 1:1-11

Luke alone among the New Testament authors (here and in his gospel for this day, 24:46-53) reports Jesus' ascension as an actual visible event that took place near Bethany (Gospel) on the Mount of Olives (Acts) and was observed by "witnesses," that is, the apostles. The event takes place in an altered state of consciousness; it is a trance experience. The Greek word in verse 10 (gazing intently at the sky) is the word Luke uses in Acts to identify a trance experience (see e.g., Acts 7:55).

There are two kinds of trance experiences: individual and group. This is a group type of experience (recall 1 Cor 15:6 where Jesus appeared to more than five hundred at one time). According to anthropological and psychiatric studies, it is not uncommon for those who have lost loved ones in death to have vivid experiences of them for up to five years after the event, and sometimes longer. While such experiences are especially common at the burial place, they can occur elsewhere, too.

Where do the deceased go at death? To use non-theological language, they go to alternate reality. All of reality consists of two parts: the one in which human beings presently live (called the world, ordinary reality, or culturally consensual reality) and the one to which human beings go after they die to join God and the spirit world (called alternate reality, or in theological terms "heaven," "with God," "the world to come," and the like). Cultures who hold this understanding of reality know that there is an entryway between the two parts of reality: ordinary and alternate. It is a hole or an opening or a crack or a door between the earth and sky which a person must find in order to go from one realm to the other. According to the sacred traditions of many cultures, that hole, crack, or door is located over the city in which is located the earthly abode of the deity. In Greek tradition, the hole was over Delphi. In the Israelite tradition, the hole is over Jerusalem. Thus, Jesus could not likely have ascended in Galilee (Matt 28:16), for the hole is not located there. Nor does Matthew say that. He says only that Jesus met the disciples there. Luke places the ascension at the most plausible place, where the passageway between this world and the sky is located in Israelite tradition, namely in the environs of Jerusalem. The two men in white robes are typical of Luke and are typical representative beings from alternate reality.

As one can expect in a trance experience, the apostles receive instruction from the risen Jesus just before he departs their company (stay in Jerusalem; wait for the Spirit; bear witness to the ends of the earth). The two messengers from alternate reality conclude the trance experience by promising them that Jesus will return.

Responsorial Psalm: 47:2-3, 6-7, 8-9

This enthronement psalm was sung in the Temple annually at the New Year feast when the Ark of the Lord was installed anew in its place. This symbolized the Lord's definitive enthronement and was met with shouts of joy and blasts on the shofar. Non-Israelites who witnessed this event recognized the superiority of Israel's God over others. Though originating in a limited nationalistic perspective, the psalm's conclusion finds its fulfillment in the first reading and the gospel (Luke 24:46-53) for today's liturgy.

Seventh Sunday of Easter
Acts 7:55-60

The Greek verb translated "looked up intently" (or "gazed") occurs just fourteen times in the New Testament. Luke uses it ten times in Acts, twice in his Gospel, and Paul uses it twice (2 Cor 3:7, 13). The use of this verb displays four important features. The subject is always a holy person, that is a *ḥasid* or *ṣaddiq* in the Israelite tradition. The person doing this activity is at prayer or in trance, an altered state of consciousness. The knowledge or intuition gained comes from alternate reality rather than an experience of this reality. Finally, this verb (used in an aorist participial form) is followed by a main verb of seeing or saying (also in the aorist, or "once for always," tense). Stephen is clearly identified as a holy man ("filled with the Holy Spirit"). He is in trance when he sees the sky open up and Jesus standing there at the right hand of God in alternate reality. He announces what he sees to the gathering, infuriating them. They drive him out of the city and stone him, laying their cloaks at the feet of Saul who witnesses Stephen's trance and death. In a very short while, driven by rage against other believers in Jesus Messiah, Saul will also experience the risen Jesus in trance (Acts 9). This is God's customary way of communicating with human beings (see 1 Sam 3:1), whether they are saintly or not.

Responsorial Psalm: 97:1-2, 6-7, 9

This postexilic psalm honors God as a just king. The verse that links this psalm with the first reading is: "all peoples see his glory" (v. 6). In the first reading, Stephen saw the glory of God in a trance experience. In these psalm verses, the glory (honor, reputation, splendor) of God is reflected in nature (mentioned in the verses omitted today), and the heavens reveal his justice. All peoples see God's glory in divine justice manifest in many different ways, whether in creation, in life, or in personal experience.

* The Vigil of Pentecost
Genesis 11:1-9

According to the biblical account, Babylon (Babel) was the first city built by humans after the flood. It is the first city of our era of humankind. The biblical story of Babylon further teaches that this is where humankind, which had been united at that time, became quite divided, and where diverse human languages originated. It was a punishment levied by God against the builders for their audacity. Extra-biblical traditions help us to fill in gaps in our high context biblical reports. Nimrod, grandson of Ham son of Noah, was the first "mighty man" on earth (Gen 10:8). Relying on the Greek translation (LXX), Philo of Alexandria noted that Nimrod began to be a "giant" on earth. He wanted to take revenge against God for flooding the earth and for killing his forefathers, so he decided to build a tower higher than the water could reach, perhaps even into the sky, the realm of God (see Josephus, *Antiquities* 1.113-114).

The Akkadian name "Babel" means the "Gate of God." Thus this city, Babylon, and its tower were intended to be the place where God and humans could meet and enter each other's territory. Since God came down to visit and look around, it seems that the technology worked (see Gen 10:8)! It is the only city in the world to which God descended to make a personal visit. But the tower, which was originally intended to maintain the unity of humankind (see v. 4), begot human discord instead. The Genesis story doesn't say why, but later, extra-biblical traditions of Israel, as noted above by Josephus, do. Nimrod's plan was set in motion in contempt of God! For this, the city would eventually be destroyed.

In Israel's history, God used this city to punish Judah. Its ruler, Nebuchadnezzar, destroyed the Temple and took the elites into Exile (see Jer 20:4). But God still intended to destroy Babylon (see Isa 14:22; 21:9). After his conquest of Persia, Alexander the Great was going to make Babylon the center of his worldwide empire, but his successors abandoned the idea and the city. By the first century C.E., Babylon was in ruins and deserted, exactly the image presented by John the Revealer (Revelation 17–20).

or Exodus 19:3-8a, 16-20b

God comes to visit humans in this reading, too. God offers to make a covenant with the Israelites. If they accept—and it is always a matter of freely accepting the offer—they will be God's special possession. They must hearken to YHWH's voice and not to the voice of any other god. The word "possession" in Hebrew and in Akkadian means "treasures of the wealthy and of the king." This sense of the word also occurs elsewhere in the Hebrew Bible (Deut 7:6; 14:2; 26:18; Ps 135:4). Scholars are not certain of the meaning of "kingdom of priests." Since the phrase occurs with "holy nation," it can be considered somewhat synonymous. If Israel agrees to God's offer, to be special to God, it will be set apart from others (basically, that is what holy means), sacred among nations as priests are among people.

Then God appears in verses 16-19. Like other theophanies in the Bible, this one takes place in a storm (see Exod 15:8, 10; Judg 5:4-5; Ps 18:6-19; 29; 77:16-20). The text actually mingles into the original event at Mount Sinai some elements of subsequent liturgical reenactments. For instance, the trumpet blast replicated the thunder; the furnace or fire pot replicated the smoke. This is how later generations repeated and celebrated this foundational experience with God. In the last verse, God establishes the mediating role of Moses by summoning him to the top of the mountain.

or Ezekiel 37:1-14

"I have promised, and I will do it, says the LORD" (v. 14). What comforting words spoken by the prophet. Ezekiel reports another of his many vision experiences, an altered state of consciousness experience. Verses 2-10 report the vision while verses 11-14 (these bones are the whole house of Israel) give the explanation. Interpretation is never easy or direct because the vision is usually not linear or sequential. This means that the visionary sees many images which have to be sorted out in the interpretation. Ezekiel sees a huge number of dead, dry bones. Whose bones are these? What do they mean? Is God going to restore dead people to life? The interpretation begins in verse 11 where God identifies the bones as Israel in Babylonian exile. God tells the prophet of the divine intent to bring these dead bones back to life, that is, to give new life to dead Israel. It is not at all a promise of restoring individual people to life.

Throughout this passage there is a play on the word "spirit" repeated in verses 1, 5, 6, 8, 9, 10, 14. The Hebrew word *ruah* can mean the wind, breath, spirit (of God in this context). In verses 2-8, no wind, breath, or spirit is present at all. In verses 9-10, Ezekiel is commanded to pray to "the spirit," and in verse 14, God finally declares: "I will put my spirit in you that you may live!" Altered states of consciousness experiences lend themselves to such fluidity of interpretation.

or Joel 3:1-5

A devastating plague of locusts coupled with a drought (perhaps in the last half of the fifth century B.C.E. and the first half of the fourth century B.C.E.) are the occasion of Joel's oracle. When both these tragedies end, Joel recognizes this as a saving deed worked by YHWH. This is a sure sign that YHWH is present in the midst of Israel. One consequence of YHWH's presence is a pouring out of God's spirit, which produces ecstatic experience (see Num 11:24-30; 1 Sam 10:10). That old men dream dreams and young men see visions may be an indication of cultural expectations concerning altered state of consciousness experiences, but not inflexibly. Moreover, there are signs in the sky that YHWH is at work rescuing Israel.

Responsorial Psalm: 104:1-2, 24, 35, 27-28, 29, 30

The refrain focuses our attention on the common element in the four readings proposed for this vigil. "Lord, send out your Spirit, and renew the face of the earth." In this psalm, the poet (a very capable master of language) reflects on creation, explaining why and how God the creator acts. The final strophe is particularly appropriate. YHWH is master of life and death. The psalmist observes the cycle of life, death, and new life which the Lord has established. It is evident in all of creation, even in the life of Israel. And it is all a gift bestowed by God's spirit.

* Pentecost
Acts 2:1-11

Luke reports yet another group type trance experience in which each member of the group becomes aware of being filled by a holy spirit. Belief in spirits was common in the ancient world, and a variety was recognized: good, malevolent, and capricious. The members here recognize that they are encountering a good or holy spirit. Luke mentions two elements of the trance: what is seen (visual) and what is heard (sound). The sound, a "noise like a strong driving wind," comes from the sky. This means it has an other-than-human source. The Israelite tradition considered thunder to be the sound of God's voice (Psalm 29; Mark 1:11), though people could differ in their interpretation of the sounds they heard (John 12:29). Since the word for wind can also mean spirit, the sound indeed is of a strong wind or spirit filling the entire home. The visual element, what everyone saw in this group trance, was "tongues as of fire." This would plausibly be a red color, perhaps tinged with yellow. In trance, colors identify the level of the trance, from light to deep. These colors indicate a deeper trance. The tongue shape of the fire quite likely relates to the result to which the vision plausibly contributes, namely, speaking in tongues (glossolalia). But the shape of a tongue also reminds one of a slit or opening between ordinary reality and alternate reality. If this is true, then the gathered community is at stage one of the trance (seeing geometric patterns), and Luke's report may already be anticipating what the community learned in stage two (searching for meaning in what is seen) or stage three (often arriving at totally unexpected insight).

Contemporary scholars familiar with the extensive research on glossolalia note that either Luke or his source misunderstood and therefore misinterpreted the phenomenon. In glossolalia, speech becomes musical sound. It is lexically noncommunicative, that is, this is not the informative or communicative side of discourse. Messages or insights are very rare. The musicality of glossolalia is a regular series of pulses of accented and unaccented syllables, and it is learned. One can imitate what one hears even at the first instance (see 2 Sam 10:5-12), though sometimes it occurs without a model to imitate. It is also possible that Luke deliberately speaks of foreign languages in his report (Acts 2:4, 8-11) in order to present this event as a reversal of the Babel experience of the confusion of languages (Genesis 11).

Notice that the devout Judeans were divided in their assessment of the event. Some thought the speakers were drunk (see v. 13), while others believed that it was of God because they were speaking of "the mighty acts of God." As with all trance experiences, interpretation is key. In this report, the audience interprets what they hear, the speakers do not interpret what they are saying. Even in the speech he makes, Peter does not interpret what was said. He identifies the experience as an authentic trance, induced by the Spirit, and then he takes the occasion to preach about Jesus.

Responsorial Psalm: 104:1, 24, 29-30, 31, 34

Some different verses are selected from the same psalm used on the Vigil of Pentecost. Again the refrain highlights the key idea: God's spirit is an agent of renewal. It is worthwhile to ask God to send forth the Spirit to renew all creation.

Trinity Sunday
Proverbs 8:22-31

This is one of the most intriguing passages in the book of Proverbs, if not in the entire Hebrew bible. Lady (or woman or dame) Wisdom explains her relationship to the LORD. Her birth is from the LORD, she existed before creation. She witnessed creation in which she played a role (artisan/crafts [wo]man? or child?). She delights and "plays" before God, yet she also delights at being involved with human beings. Who is this woman? The late Fr. Roland Murphy, respected expert in Wisdom literature, proposed that she is a surrogate for YHWH. More specifically, she represents the "feminine" in God when the first human beings were created in the divine image and likeness: "male and female he created them" (Gen 1:27). Human intelligence, which shares in this facet of the deity, is indeed creative. Human intelligence provides countless moments and kinds of delight in every dimension of human activity. On this feast of the Holy Trinity, as believers reflect on the richness of God who requires three persons in which to express the deity, this mystery helps humans appreciate the similar mystery of their being which brought God delight in creating it.

Responsorial Psalm: 8:4-5, 6-7, 8-9

Verses 5-7 constitute a splendid response to the speech of Lady Wisdom. The Hebrew words for "man" and "son of man" are inclusive of men and women. They could be appropriately rendered "humans" and "mere mortals" (as in the 1991 revised NAB Psalter). How wonderful indeed is God who shared the deity's finest qualities with human creatures.

Eleventh Sunday
in Ordinary Time
2 Samuel 12:7-10, 13

This is one of the few prophetic judgment speeches directed to an individual in the Hebrew Bible. Yet it is so embedded in the narrative that the original form has probably been lost. God has commissioned Nathan the prophet to speak to David (v. 1). Verses 7-8 recount God's blessing to David, and are followed by a generic and theological accusation (v. 9a): David spurned the Lord and did Evil. This is quite likely not the original form of the accusation. The prophets were more direct, as the next sentences explain: David had Uriah murdered, then took his wife with whom he had already committed adultery. Verse 10 announces the judgment, but the original form is likely in verse 11 because it begins in typical form: "thus says the LORD." Nevertheless, the point of this redacted text segment is clear. It relates well to the gospel (Luke 7:36–8:3) in which Jesus tells a parable that serves as his vehicle for rendering prophetic judgment against an individual.

Responsorial Psalm: 32:1-2, 5, 7, 11

This is the first of seven penitential psalms. In verses not used today, the point of the psalm becomes clearer. The psalmist's real problem was dissimulation. When he refused to acknowledge his sin, his body was wracked with illness. Once he admitted it (v. 5), the Lord was forgiving. From this experience, he exhorts listeners to be glad and exult appropriately.

81

Twelfth Sunday
in Ordinary Time
Zechariah 12:10-11; 13:1

Verses 9-14 from which today's reading has been excerpted are in the form of a mourning rite. All of Jerusalem is mourning, but for whom? That is a very problematic verse in its context, despite the fact that John 19:33-37 and Revelation 1:7 identify the pierced one with Jesus. The Hebrew is less clear on that point. The phrase "they shall look on him" literally is "they shall look to me," which expresses conversion, turning to God. But how can God be pierced except metaphorically? Yet if that sense is followed, how would one mourn for God? NAB follows most translations, but the one pierced (now a human being) is still difficult if not impossible to identify. The mourning, however, will be very great. It will remind one of pagan mourning rites for the death of Hadad, a storm god, but perhaps the sacred author really means Adonis/Tammuz, since mourning rites are usually associated with a fertility god.

In spite of this difficulty, the thrust of the passage is clear. God takes the initiative by instilling a new spirit in the people, one that flows from repentance for their "sins and uncleanness." Repentance for whatever the specific but unidentifiable sin was brings forgiveness symbolized by the fountain. In the gospel (Luke 9:18-24), Jesus speaks of his suffering, death, and vindication, and notes that his followers too must take up the cross daily. All can expect to be pierced.

Responsorial Psalm: 63:2, 3-4, 5-6, 8-9

The yearning for God reflected in today's selected verses finds fulfillment and satisfaction in the final stanza. The psalmist is standing near the ark and feels embraced by God in mystical ecstasy, an image perhaps suggested by the ark which is embraced in the wings of the cherubim (Exod 25:20-21).

Thirteenth Sunday in Ordinary Time
1 Kings 19:16b, 19-21

This story tells how Elisha succeeds Elijah as prophet. The transfer of power and authority from Elijah to Elisha echoes the same kind of transfer from Moses to Joshua (Num 27:18-23; Deut 34:9). Elisha thus is presented as a model of the Mosaic prophet (Deut 18:15-21). Elisha's request to bid farewell to his parents is similar to an experience of Jesus in today's gospel (Luke 9:51-62). It would seem that in both cases, the request is rebuffed, and the petitioner heeds the call. Elisha's slaughtering of his oxen and distributing them to his people to eat quite likely symbolizes putting aside his former way of life. However, it also illustrates two cultural points. His obedience to the divine call (given through Elijah) is exemplary, and distributing his slain oxen to his people is precisely the proper thing to do in a culture convinced that all goods of life are finite in quantity and already distributed. Rather than putting it into a retirement account, the Middle Easterner distributes surplus immediately. And Elisha became Elijah's successor as prophet.

Responsorial Psalm: 16:1-2, 5, 7-8, 9-10, 11

This lament of a Levite suffering physical ailment is full of confidence. Since Levites had no landed property, they could sing: "You are my inheritance, O Lord," expressing total dependence upon God. The refrain eventually became appropriate for all Israelites, for God said "the land is mine, and you are but aliens who have become my tenants" (Lev 25:23). Peter quotes verses 8-11 when preaching about the resurrection of Jesus (Acts 2:24-28). In today's liturgy, the sentiments of this psalm link the first reading with the gospel by offering a vision of what will result after obediently and faithfully following the divine invitation.

Fourteenth Sunday in Ordinary Time
Isaiah 66:10-14c

These verses from the final chapter of Third Isaiah express sentiments of joy and salvation. The theme of joy and rejoicing permeates Third Isaiah (46:7; 10:18; 61:3, 7, 10; 65:13-19). The prophet focuses on a restored Jerusalem using feminine imagery since cities in antiquity were viewed as feminine. Then the imagery switches to God perceived as mother (see also 42:14; 45:10; 49:15). The conclusion is self-evident. Such nourishment will promote growth, and through it all, "the LORD's power shall be known to his servants." Perhaps one idea that links this reading to the gospel (Luke 10:1-2, 17-20) is the exhortation to disciples to "eat what is set before you" when they travel on their ministry. God will look after them.

Responsorial Psalm: 66:1-3, 4-5, 6-7, 16, 20

This psalm reflects the Judaic tradition of "contextualizing" (to use a modern term) an ancient tradition to a present situation. The topic is the mighty works of God, specifically the Exodus (vv. 6-7), but the notion is being applied to the psalmist's situation, which is totally unknown to the modern reader. The shift from plurals to the singular in verses 16 and 20 reflects the typical thinking pattern of collectivistic individuals who derive their strength and identity from the group. Boundaries between the two are blurred, and the individual can appropriate what the group has experienced. The note of joy in this psalm (echoes in the refrain) links the first reading with today's gospel.

Fifteenth Sunday in Ordinary Time
Deuteronomy 30:10-14

The book of Deuteronomy was likely incorporated into the Pentateuch by "P" in the post-exilic period. Thus the sentiments here clearly reflect the thinking of Jeremiah 31:33 and Ezekiel 36:26-27. God's law is not esoteric or out of reach. God has placed it in the very hearts of human beings who have only to carry it out. It is a guide to meaningful life, to the practicalities of daily life. The law is the way of life for God's people. One link with today's gospel (Luke 10:25-37) is the notion of heart. The scholar who questioned Jesus "had no heart," missed Jesus' point, and was interested only in tripping Jesus up (testing him).

Responsorial Psalm: 69:14, 17, 30-31, 36, 37

This is the prayer of a very sick person who manages to maintain strong confidence that God will respond to his prayer. Today's selected verses omit those which hurl a curse against the psalmist's enemies (vv. 23-29). The selection concludes instead with the optimistic sentiments. The Lord hears those who have temporarily lost their rightful status (poor, imprisoned). Moreover, God will restore the good fortune of Judah so that those who "love his name" (or keep his commandments as the Deuteronomist exhorts) shall inherit and inhabit it. This selection admirably links the first reading with the gospel (Luke 10:25-27), in which the legal scholar was more interested in shaming Jesus than in keeping the commandments.

or Psalm 19:8, 9, 10, 11

These verses clearly praise the Torah, which is not at all viewed as a burden but rather as enlightenment for leading a good life, pleasing to God. The psalmist indeed uses God's name, YHWH, and describes God's instruction as sweeter than syrup or honey.

Sixteenth Sunday in Ordinary Time
Genesis 18:1-10a

In the heat of the day, Abraham falls into an altered state of consciousness in which he learns from the LORD that Sarah will finally bear a son next year. In his trance experience, Abraham with the aid of Sarah extends hospitality to three strangers who are surrogates for YHWH. This is fully in accord with the rules of Middle Eastern hospitality. By definition, hospitality is extended almost exclusively by men exclusively to strangers. It is not extended to family and friends. To them one extends steadfast, loving kindness (*ḥesed* in Hebrew). The purpose of hospitality is to provide safe passage through dangerous territory. Travel in the ancient world was considered deviant, and travelers were suspected of being devious. Only through the graces of a local person could travelers expect safe passage.

Hospitality involved three stages. First, the potential host tests the strangers to determine whether to allow them into his household. This is lacking in today's report. If Abraham is not living in a village or city and this is desert, it may be less the need for safeguarding the strangers from hostile villagers than the honor-bound duty to help a traveler through the desert. In the second stage, the host determines to transform the strangers into guests. Clearly Abraham has decided to do this, seemingly without hesitation. Both host and guest are now bound by rules guiding proper behavior. Abraham and

Sarah provide all the services required in hospitality. In the third and final stage, the host and guest should part as friends, but might part as enemies. In this report, the announcement of the birth of a son in the coming year clearly indicates they part as friends.

Notice that Abraham serves an unkosher combination of steer, curds, and milk, mixing dairy and meat products. This event takes place, of course, before such laws were promulgated. Further, considering how long it takes to butcher and prepare a steer, this is a far cry from a snack or fast food. Finally, it would be an insult to the host to attempt to repay hospitality. Since God alone is the author of life, the announcement of a son is pure gift (grace) on God's part. One of the purposes of trance experiences is to learn a new direction in life. With the knowledge that he will have a son, the actualization of God's previous promise and Abraham's destiny foretold earlier becomes clearer and more imminent.

The link between this reading and today's gospel (Luke 10:38-42) intended by the architects of the Lectionary is infelicitous. Since Mary and Martha are already friends of Jesus, this is not hospitality but rather steadfast, loving kindness. The link, therefore, is quite superficial and based on a misunderstanding of Middle Eastern hospitality.

Responsorial Psalm: 15:2-3, 3-4, 5

The key idea in these psalm verses is justice, specifically "doing justice." In Middle Eastern culture, this value belongs to the social institution known as patronage. A person with surplus is bound to share it, though the choice of recipient is entirely his and can be—and often is—based on personal whim. He must give to the needy, but it need not be to the neediest! Thus, the psalm verses present for the modern believer a model of how to be a patron, or how to act justly and walk blamelessly. It is an expansion on Abraham's behavior as well as that of Mary and Martha. At the same time, God "out-patrons" Abraham, and Jesus fine tunes justice in the kin group (which is the model upon which patronage is based) with his comment to Martha.

Seventeenth Sunday
in Ordinary Time
Genesis 18:20-32

This reading is linked with the gospel by the notion of importunity. Probably most if not all readers are familiar with this story about Abraham "haggling" with God that Sodom and Gomorrah be spared. Westerners typically view haggling as "taking advantage of the other." This is not the case in Middle Eastern culture. The fact is that both parties know at the beginning it is a done deal. Abraham will make his point and win, God will capitulate. No one loses because both parties know the desired outcome. Critical to this process is the phrase "for the sake of." Under ordinary circumstances, one person tries to persuade the other "for the sake of your father" or "for the sake of my father." The present context in which this phrase is repeated reminds the "superior" (God) of what the deity has to gain in the process. God is reminded of "justice," that is, the value of responsibility based on kinship relationships. "Should not the judge of all the world act with justice?" Justice in Middle Eastern culture is rooted in kinship obligations. One must be faithful to kin no matter what! Abraham is speaking on behalf of God's human creatures and reminding God that they are kin. God created them! God appropriately gets the point and agrees to Abraham's bargain. Nevertheless, this was a fait accompli from the very beginning of the haggling. The link with the gospel (Luke 11:1-13) is also importunity in the context of friendship, which is extended kinship.

Responsorial Psalm: 138:1-2, 2-3, 6-7, 7-8

The key word in these select verses is "kindness" (v. 2). It translates the Hebrew *ḥesed* (steadfast, loving kindness), which is a value in the kinship context. This value eminently characteristic of God is what explains the psalmist's statement: "when I called you answered me." In the Mediterranean world, kin cannot and will not ignore kin. Two important concepts emerge here. One, what an incredible thought to realize one is kin with God. Two, this fact guarantees a positive response to one's petition. The ideas are present in both readings.

Eighteenth Sunday in Ordinary Time
Ecclesiastes 1:2; 2:21-23

The Hebrew word *ḥebel,* translated here as "vanity," has a broad range of meaning: futility, absurdity, meaninglessness, and the like. It is also translated "breath," since concretely the word means vapor or mist. Settling on the precise meaning will always depend on context. Verse 1 is repeated in 12:8, forming an inclusion. In between these verses, the sentiment is repeated often enough that if one began reading with skepticism, the reader is likely to be convinced of Qohelet's assertion at the end.

In today's reading, the focus is Qohelet's reflection on toil or labor. It can and often indeed is drudgery, but the laborer is frequently unable to keep it for personal use. Instead it is passed over to someone who didn't work for it and might not even deserve it. The reflection relates well to Jesus' statement and parable about possessions in today's gospel (Luke 12:13-21).

Responsorial Psalm: 90:3-4, 5-6, 12-13

In these verses the psalmist reflects upon the fragile nature of life. We are here today but may be gone tomorrow. The psalmist, however, prays for the grace to respond to the voice of God when it should be heard. He also prays that God "prosper the work of our hands," even though its rewards be uncertain or eventually lost, as the first reading and gospel remind us.

Nineteenth Sunday in Ordinary Time
Wisdom 18:6-9

This late-first-century B.C.E. reflection upon ancient traditions was written to strengthen the faith of Israelites who were tempted by new ideas in Alexandria and were actually abandoning their faith. Today's verses are part of a longer reflection on the tenth plague and the Exodus by which God punished Egypt but glorified and delivered Israel (18:5–19:22). It was not that the patriarchs knew the Passover in advance, but rather they received God's oath to deliver their descendants (e.g., Gen 15:13-14). Patiently did the chosen people await their redemption and just retribution for their enemies, while they celebrated the Passover ("sacrifice") in secret. The patient fidelity implied in this reading is explicitly urged by Jesus in today's gospel (Luke 22:32-48).

Responsorial Psalm: 33:1, 12, 18-19, 20-22

The verses selected from this hymn sing the praises of God who from heaven looks out for the chosen people. Verse 20 forms an appropriate bridge between the first reading and the gospel by urging patient vigilance. The final verse is also the conclusion of the *Te Deum*.

Twentieth Sunday in Ordinary Time
Jeremiah 38:4-6, 8-10

Jeremiah's unwavering prophetic message was that Judah should surrender to Babylon and live rather than resist and die. It ran counter to governmental policy, indeed was considered treason. Jeremiah believed this was the will of God which he discerned. Though the face-off is between Jeremiah and king Zedekiah, it is clearly the princes who wield power. They persuade the weak king to dispose of Jeremiah. The princes cast him into a deep cistern to die very likely through neglect. This is what an enemy of the government, a traitor, deserves. After a while a mysterious figure, Ebed-melech (which means servant of the king), a court official, convinces this weak king to rescue Jeremiah. We know nothing of this servant, but his intervention suggests Jeremiah had friends in high places, in the very court of the king. Quite likely these powerful friends (see Jer 26:17, 24; 36:19) preferred Jeremiah's plan to that of the princes. For some unknown reason, they could not convince the king of Jeremiah's plan. Now they dispatch Ebed-melech to plea on behalf of Jeremiah, which he does successfully. The death sentence is reversed. The voice of the prophet and his challenging, unpatriotic message will continue to be heard. The discord occasioned by Jeremiah and his prophetic message is exactly what Jesus says his own message will occasion in today's gospel (Luke 12:49-53).

Responsorial Psalm: 40:2, 3, 4, 18

Though we do not know why the composer of this psalm was punished as he was, the description of his fate sounds very similar to Jeremiah's (see also Ps 69:1-2). In the psalmist's case, he may have been imprisoned somewhere in the temple cisterns. The Lord set his feet on solid ground (perhaps inspired by the rock of sacrifice—see Ps 27:5). The concluding verses express trust in God such as Jeremiah surely had and Jesus certainly hoped for among his followers.

Twenty-First Sunday in Ordinary Time
Isaiah 66:18-21

As anyone familiar with the Mediterranean cultural context of the Bible might expect, glory (v. 19) helps to understand these verses. God's glory, honor, reputation will be witnessed by all the world. God will send "fugitives," that is, those who returned from Exile (survivors), to Israelites living in all parts of the world. They shall bring these Israelites back to Jerusalem in a ritual procession from all directions: southern Spain (Tarshish), Africa (Put and Lud), and so on. Nations will recognize God's reputation as a faithful protector and redeemer of the chosen people. So, too, does Jesus in today's gospel (Luke 13:22-30) echo these sentiments.

Responsorial Psalm: 117: 1, 2

This shortest of all the psalms in the Psalter expresses the reason why everyone ought to marvel at, indeed praise God. The two outstanding qualities of God which justify unshakable confidence are steadfast, loving kindness *(ḥesed)* and loyalty or fidelity *(ᶜemet)*. The social context of each word is kinship, meaning God is like kin hence can be expected to behave like a kinsperson. In the Middle East, one can always rely on one's kin.

Twenty-Second Sunday in Ordinary Time
Sirach 3:17-18, 20, 28-29

In Middle Eastern culture, humility consists in setting one-self perhaps a step behind where one rightfully belongs in status. The one who practices such humility will never risk overstepping status or claiming more honor than is deserved. That would be shameful. Further, others perceive that one is not grasping for honors. That allows them the opportunity to invite such a humble person to his rightful status. The reason why such a one will be loved more than a giver of gifts is the latter puts beneficiaries in his debt. Every gift expects a gift in return. Thus sometimes it is wise to decline a gift. The link with today's gospel (Luke 14:1, 7-14) is clear, though Proverbs 25:6-7 might have been more appropriate.

(It is not clear why verses 28 and 29 were included in this reading. Verse 28 does not follow smoothly after verse 20, and verse 29 is unrelated in concept to verse 28.)

Responsorial Psalm: 68:4-5, 6-7, 10-11

With roots in Saul's reign, this psalm has a long history of use and "fine tuning" so that it is one of the most textually corrupt of all psalms. These verses speak both of the Exodus (leading prisoners to prosperity) and of settlement in Canaan (the bountiful autumnal rains). The sentiment is that God does indeed look after the poor, those who put their trust entirely in God. A humble person (Sirach) and one who invites to a banquet guests who cannot repay (Luke) manifest this kind of trust.

Twenty-Third Sunday in Ordinary Time
Wisdom 9:13-18b

This is the third section of Solomon's prayer for wisdom (Wis 9:1-18), which is this sacred author's version of what the Deuteronomic historian recorded (1 Kgs 3:6-9). Like the rest of this book, this passage, too, is well constructed literarily. An *inclusio* (repetition of words/ideas: "know counsel") identifies the beginning and end of the passage, which forms a discrete unit. Solomon notes that no human being can possibly understand God's counsel, that is what God would like people to do. The reason is that human deliberations are uncertain (timid) and earthbound. Only God can bestow true understanding. The reading very likely is intended to relate, loosely to be sure, to the latter part of today's gospel concerning deliberation (Luke 14:25-33).

Responsorial Psalm: 90:3-4, 5-6, 12-13, 14-17

Verses 12-13 form the best link between the first reading and the gospel: teach us to take our lives into serious account that we might be truly wise. The preceding verses describe the fragility of human life, while the final verse prays that God watch over the deeds and activities of human beings.

Twenty-Fourth Sunday in Ordinary Time
Exodus 32:7-11, 13-14

This report from the Elohist describes an angry God threatening to destroy the chosen people and to replace them with Moses' family. Moses, true to Mediterranean cultural fashion, appeals to God's sense of honor and reputation. How would it look especially to the Egyptians if God were to destroy these chosen people who were redeemed in such startling ways? Moreover, what about God's promise to the Patriarchs? How would it look if God reneged on these promises? So God gives in and does not punish the people.

The simple tale is rife with problems for a Western reader who might also be theologically sophisticated. Can God really be swayed by such silly arguments? Why should God care about honor and reputation? Why did God make such a bad choice to begin with, if these people turned out to be unfaithful? It is important to remember the familiar medieval scholastic dictum: "Everything human beings know and say about God is based on human experience (all theology is analogy)." Further, all human experience is culturally conditioned. God conceived and understood in Mediterranean cultural terms must be sensitive to the divine honor and reputation. Once one accepts this, the rest of the story—indeed the entire Bible—make better "Mediterranean" sense. To translate its message into another culture is a challenging but not impossible enterprise. The challenge is perhaps even greater if one wants to understand and present God in a different cultural image. The link between this reading and today's gospel (Luke 15:1-32) is readily apparent. The father in that story behaves just as God does, or perhaps more correctly, God is imagined to behave just like that Mediterranean father does in real life. The proper cultural response to aggrieved honor is obvious, but also carries unbearable consequences. The course chosen in each selection is the "humane" thing to do (if one might apply that notion to God).

Responsorial Psalm: 51:3-4, 12-13, 17, 19

This penitential psalm is among the most familiar of the entire Psalter. Its use in today's liturgy seems to be less a bridge between reading than an actual response to the first reading and the gospel. Indeed, the architects of the Lectionary assign a verse from the gospel at the response (Luke 15:18). The psalmist confesses his offense, sin, guilt, and begs for mercy. In Mediterranean culture, to beg for mercy is to ask that person to do what they know then can and should do. Nothing need be spelled out in great detail. Both know the parameters. The psalmist further requests a total "make over"; he desires a new spirit. He wants to return to well being as a totally integrated and well-balanced person. He concludes with confidence that God will accept his contrition and indeed act mercifully toward him.

Twenty-Fifth Sunday in Ordinary Time
Amos 8:4-7

Amos, the first of the "classical prophets," that is, those whose statements were recorded in the form of a written collection, lived in a period of unimaginable material prosperity for Israel, the northern kingdom (approximately 786 to 742 B.C.E.). It was a profitable lull between two powerful appearances of Assyria on the Middle Eastern scene. In these verses, Amos rails against hypocrisy. Those who purposefully defraud the poor and needy also take care to observe the holy days ("new moon"). The prophet identifies their well-known strategy: they will use false measures *(ephah)* and weights (shekel in this instance is a measure of weight). Moreover, they will take their debtors as slaves ("buy the lowly for silver . . . the poor for a pair of sandals") and sell to the needy that which only animals would eat. The Lord of course will not forget such injustice. It is unfortunate that this reading has been linked with today's gospel (Luke 16:1-13) in which the steward acted shrewdly but perhaps not dishonestly (see *The Cultural World of Jesus: Sunday by Sunday, Cycle C*).

Responsorial Psalm: 113:1-2, 4-6, 7-8

This psalm begins the collection known as the "Egyptian Hallel" (Psalms 113–118), which were sung on the first day of each month ("the new moon"). This is likely one reason why the psalm was selected as a response to the reading from Amos. Of course, an obvious second reason can be found in verses 7-8 recognizing God as redeemer of the poor such as those defrauded in Amos' ancient Israel.

Twenty-Sixth Sunday in Ordinary Time
Amos 6:1a, 4-7

Zion (Jerusalem) in verse 1a is a puzzle since Amos prophesied in Israel not Judah. However, prophets never lost sight of the united kingdom, and their messages though directed at one kingdom could at times be equally applicable to the other. Amos' condemnation of the wealthy is rooted in their refusal to acknowledge the threats to, indeed the imminent collapse of, Israel. It is important to keep in mind the Middle Eastern understanding of wealth. In itself, there is nothing wrong with wealth, but the Middle Eastern expectation is that such people will share their surplus, will become "patrons" to needy clients. When the wealthy do not share, then it is appropriate to translate the words "wealthy" or "rich" by "greedy" (see Luke 12:15). The link with today's gospel (Luke 16:19-31) is clear.

Responsorial Psalm: 146:7, 8-9, 9-10

This is the first of a series of "Hallel" or praise psalms that conclude the Psalter. The verses selected for today's liturgy echo the events of the Exodus. Restoring "sight to the blind" in verse 8 is an idiom for freeing captives (see Isa 42:7; 61:1). "Strangers, fatherless, widows" are also Exodus references (22:20-21). But as is the practice in the Hebraic tradition, ancient texts are always appropriated to contemporary concerns, often with disregard for the original historical setting. Thus, God is faithful (loyal) to the needy and to those who behave justly. The psalm serves well to link the first reading and the gospel.

Twenty-Seventh Sunday in Ordinary Time
Habakkuk 1:2-3; 2:2-4

"Violence" is a key word in Habakkuk (1:3, 9; 2:8, 17 [twice]) and refers to inhumane treatment of human beings. The prophet's lament directed to God is "Why doesn't God do something about it?" The deity's passivity suggests approval! Habakkuk is quite angry. God's reply (2:2-4) comes in a trance experience, an altered state of consciousness. The instruction to "write it down" is typical, since visionaries—indeed all human beings—must write their inspirations down as soon as possible after they occur lest the visionary forget or the insight become vague. God assures the prophet that what he will see will certainly come to pass, but in God's good time. The prophet and his people must wait patiently ("if it delays, wait for it"). The final verse: "The just one, because of his loyalty [the most appropriate cultural translation of 'faith'], shall live." If one remains patiently loyal to God, everything will work out as God wills it. This verse, of course, is the link with today's gospel (Luke 17:5-10).

Responsorial Psalm: 95:1-2, 6-7, 8-9

The repetition of "today" in these verses and this psalm gives a ring of urgency to its message. Pilgrims to Jerusalem come into the sanctuary, as far as the Holy of Holies, and they prostrate themselves. The composer links this pilgrimage with the Exodus and brings forward a reminder to those present "harden not your hearts." They must take to heart what they have heard, just as contemporary worshipers ought to do.

Twenty-Eighth Sunday in Ordinary Time
2 Kings 5:14-17

Leprosy, or Hansen's disease as we know it today, is nowhere discussed in the Bible. The Hebrew and Greek words used are not the words for "true" leprosy. Neither are any of the symptoms listed characteristic of leprosy. The problem is instead a visible skin condition of some kind which was amenable to a nonmedical remedy. In this report about Naaman, it is important to know that Elisha is described as a "man of God." All cultures recognize such a person who has regular and intimate contact with the spirit world and the deity. The major function of such a person is to mediate healing from that world to needy human beings. Indeed, that is Naaman's confession, that "there is no God in all the earth, except in Israel."

A second important cultural point in this story concerns the offer of a gift. In many, though not all, cultures, healing is "free." The holy man ought not to be paid, since the healing is from God and not from the holy man. Naaman's offer is well intended. He wants to express his indebtedness. Elisha's refusal is proper. God should get the glory. At the end, God indeed does since Naaman becomes a worshiper back in his own country. The link with the Gospel (Luke 17:11-19) is clear. (For additional information about leprosy see *The Cultural World of Jesus: Sunday by Sunday, Cycle C*, pp. 148–51.)

Responsorial Psalm: 98:1, 2-3, 3-4

Another psalm acclaiming Yʜᴡʜ as King over all the universe. All the nations and all the ends of the earth witness Yʜᴡʜ's mighty deeds on behalf of Israel. In today's first reading, however, a foreigner personally experiences God's salvation, redemption from his illness. This psalm serves as a most appropriate link between the first reading and the gospel, both of which highlight the good fortune of a foreigner.

Twenty-Ninth Sunday in Ordinary Time
Exodus 17:8-13

The Amalekites are a fierce tribe near Kadesh in the Negeb (see Gen 14:7; Num 13:29; 14:25). They controlled the caravan routes between Egypt and Arabia. The Israelites defeat them because YHWH fights on their side as long as Moses extends over his people the rod he used to defeat the Pharaoh. Still, Moses is at the center of this legend. Readers are to be edified by Moses as a true human hero. As long as Moses is faithful in keeping in his hands steady, the Israelites prevail. Such stamina, even with the aid of Aaron and Hur, is fitting for a hero like Moses. This reading is probably intended to relate to Jesus' advice in the gospel (Luke 18:1-8) "to pray always without becoming weary."

Responsorial Psalm: 121:1-2, 3-4, 5-6, 7-8

This psalm might have been a blessing spoken by a priest to inspire confidence in a pilgrim about to begin his journey home from a pilgrimage to the Temple. Even traveling in a caravan was risky, but less so than traveling alone, which would be suicide. The imagery of these verses make good sense in such a scenario. The priest insists that God is ever vigilant, never sleeping, but always playing the role of "guardian of Israel."

Thirtieth Sunday
in Ordinary Time
Sirach 35:12-14, 16-18

The parallelism between the words in verses 12-14 (weak; literally the poor, the oppressed, the orphan, and the widow) reminds us what these groups have in common. Each has experienced a temporary loss of status or honor which is the essential definition of "poor" in the Bible (rarely if ever an economic designation). The state can pass, and indeed whoever has the misfortune of falling into that state is obliged to extricate him/herself from it. A widow can remarry, an orphan can be adopted, one who loses status can regain it. These verses emphasize that it is God who redeems from these conditions.

The sentiments of verses 16-18 explain what makes prayer effective. God hears the lowly (or one bitterly distressed) because such a one is persistent and does not desist until God responds. Sirach seems to draw upon Lamentation 3:44 for his imagery: "You [God] wrapped yourself in a cloud / which prayer could not pierce." The lowly one who serves God faithfully does not cease until his prayer "pierces the clouds . . . reaches its goal . . . and the Most High responds, / judges justly, and affirms the right." Today's gospel (Luke 18:9-14) illustrates the prayer of a lowly person.

Responsorial Psalm: 34:2-3, 17-18, 19, 23

This entire acrostic (alphabetical) psalm revolves around the principle that God rewards good people but punishes evil people. Verses 17-18 enunciate the principle explicitly, while the refrain (v. 7a) echoes the first reading and helps link it to the gospel.

Thirty-First Sunday in Ordinary Time
Wisdom 11:22–12:2

The heart of the sage's message here is that God is merciful because God loves all creation. God would not create hateful things. The fact that God's creative spirit is in all things is what spares them from God's wrath. Moreover, because God can do all things, God is certainly capable of showing mercy. The thought that God rebukes sinners little by little so that they may repent is similar to the sentiments expressed in 2 Maccabees 6:12-17. Recalling that all prayer is a form of communication intended to influence or persuade another person to the petitioner's request, it is easy to understand the sage's use of flattery toward God: "O LORD and lover of souls." In the gospel (Luke 19:1-10), Jesus affirms Zacchaeus as already having obtained God's forgiveness.

Responsorial Psalm: 145:1-2, 8-9, 10-11, 13, 14

Verse 8 of this alphabetical psalm plainly echoes the first reading: "the LORD is . . . slow to anger and of great kindness." God also lifts the weak and raises up the oppressed. For this reason all should praise God by expressing their indebtedness for kindness received.

Thirty-Second Sunday in Ordinary Time
2 Maccabees 7:1-2, 9-14

This familiar story from the Maccabean period is the sequel to the torture and death of Eleazar, who intended by his own manly death to "leave to the young a noble example of how to die willingly and generously for the revered and holy laws" (2 Macc 6:28). His example is immediately followed by the story of the martyrdom of the seven sons whose unnamed mother encouraged them to remain faithful to Judaism and not betray it even to escape a torturous death. She was put to death after her sons. The statement of each son in today's reading adds another concept to that which preceded. The second son declares that God will raise them up (v. 9). The third son adds that they will rise with integral bodies despite the mutilation that is killing them (v. 11). The fourth son notes that the wicked will not share in the resurrection (compare Dan 12:2; 1 Thess 4:13-18). The link with today's gospel (Luke 20:27-38) is, of course, that Jesus shares this Judaic belief in resurrection while his Sadducee opponents do not.

Responsorial Psalm: 17:1, 5-6, 8, 15

It is verse 15 in particular that bridges the first reading with the gospel: "I . . . shall behold your face" and "I shall be content in your presence." The late Old Testament expert Fr. Carroll Stuhlmueller, whose inspiring reflections on the psalms remain ever fresh, correctly noted that these phrases refer primarily to the Temple liturgy. "To see God's face" is a way of describing a visit to the Temple (Exod 23:17; Ps 42:1-5). Moreover, liturgical ceremonies were expected to lead one intimately into God's presence ("shadow of your wings" probably refers to the wings of the cherubim and God's presence with Israel; Exod 25:20-22). The Septuagint (Greek translation of the Hebrew) explicitly interpreted "on waking" as a reference to resurrection (see Isa 26:19; Dan 12:2) by adding the phrase: "in the vision of your glory." That would seem to be the sense intended by today's liturgy as well.

Thirty-Third Sunday in Ordinary Time
Malachi 3:19-20a

The link between this reading and the gospel for this Sunday (Luke 21:5-19) is quite likely "the day [that] is coming" (Mal 3:19) and "the days will come" (Luke 21:6). Malachi describes that day of reckoning for the wicked in terms of a blazing fire (oven) which will reduce them to ashes. A second image that he uses for the just is "sun of justice." In general, Israel made few references to the sun in its literature, since it was worshiped by most of her neighboring nations. Egypt worshiped a sun god in the shape of a winged solar dish. In Persian thought, fiery consummation characterized the end times. Malachi may be reflecting such influences. Still, Israel did associate God with the sun ("The LORD let his face shine upon you," Num 6:24-26). Upon the righteous in Israel, the sun of righteousness will cast its healing rays.

Responsorial Psalm: 98:5-6, 7-8, 9

Verse 9 is the plausible bridge between the first reading and today's gospel. It is, of course, accommodated in the liturgy. On the other hand, it is difficult to deny the universal sweep of verse 9: God comes to rule the earth, the world, the peoples. It may perhaps have been a flash of "accidental" ("providential"?) insight for the psalmist, whose creative spirit was overwhelmed with optimism.

Thirty-Fourth Sunday
in Ordinary Time
(Christ the King)
2 Samuel 5:1-3

The obvious theme is "king" to accommodate this feast. Accommodation is commonly practiced in the liturgy. Still, according to Church guidelines for interpreting Scripture, all are obliged to use historical critical methods to interpret the Bible. So the superficial link between this reading and the gospel is simply "king." Noted biblical scholar James Flanagan offers interesting insight into these verses. The story line of 1–2 Samuel makes it clear that David accepts divinely authorized leadership over Israel with reluctance. Tension between the houses of Saul and David lie at the basis of David's uneasiness. This passage has been redacted by at least three hands, so it has been interpreted and reinterpreted. (Notice the report in v. 3: they come to King David to anoint him king of Israel. Was he already a king elsewhere?) The simple point is when leadership crises among agrarians arise, as it has here between northern and southern coalitions in ancient Palestine, the principals often seek a leader from among neighboring nomadic groups to resolve the crises. Thus the leaders of the tribes of Israel come to David, who might have been a Philistine chieftain according to John McKenzie, to be their new leader. Since he accepts, they anoint him. The link with today's gospel (Luke 23:35-43) is clear, but see the comments on this feast in *The Cultural World of Jesus: Sunday by Sunday, Cycle C* (169).

Responsorial Psalm: 122:1-2, 3-4, 4-5

These verses selected from one of the Songs of Zion praise the (now vacant) throne and traditions of David. It is not transparently clear how the psalm bridges the first reading with the gospel. The architects of the liturgy have worked an accommodation here which worshipers are challenged to uncover.

Recommended Readings

Old Testament

Craghan, John F. *Psalms for All Seasons.* Collegeville: The Liturgical Press, 1993.

Gottwald, Norman K. *The Hebrew Bible: A Socio-Literary Introduction.* Minneapolis: Fortress Press, 1985.

Holladay, William L. *Long Ago God Spoke: How Christians May Hear the Old Testament Today.* Minneapolis: Fortress Press, 1995.

Stuhlmueller, Carroll. *Psalms.* 2 vols. Old Testament Message. Wilmington, Del.: Michael Glazier, 1983.

____. *The Spirituality of the Psalms.* Collegeville: The Liturgical Press, 2002.

Cultural World of the Bible

Pilch, John J. *The Cultural Dictionary of the Bible.* Collegeville: The Liturgical Press, 1999.

____. *The Cultural World of Jesus: Sunday by Sunday, Cycle C.* Collegeville: The Liturgical Press, 1997.

____. *The Cultural World of the Apostles: The Second Reading, Sunday by Sunday, Year C.* Collegeville: The Liturgical Press, 2003.

_____. *The Triduum: Breaking Open the Scriptures.* Collegeville: The Liturgical Press, 2000.

Pilch, John J., and Bruce J. Malina, eds. *Handbook of Biblical Social Values.* Peabody, Mass.: Hendrickson Publishers, 1998.

Websites

Roman Catholic Lectionary for Mass:
http://clawww.lmu.edu/faculty/fjust/Lectionary.htm

Revised Common Lectionary:
http://divinity.library.vanderbilt.edu/lectionary

Cultural World of Jesus Cycle C
http://www.liturgy.slu.edu